GOLF GAMES
WITHIN
THE GAME

GOLF GAMES WITHIN THE GAME

200 Fun Ways Players Can Add Variety
and Challenge to Their Game

• • •

LINDA VALENTINE
AND MARGIE HUBBARD

Illustrated by Ben Boyd

A PERIGEE BOOK

Perigee Books
are published by
The Putnam Publishing Group
200 Madison Avenue
New York, NY 10016

First Perigee Edition 1992

Library of Congress Cataloging-in-Publication Data
Valentine, Linda, date.
Golf games within the game : 200 fun ways players can add variety
and challenge to their game / Linda Valentine and Margie Hubbard ;
illustrations by Ben Boyd.
p. cm.
Originally published by the authors in 1987.
Includes index.
ISBN 0-399-51762-6
1. Golf. 2. Golf—Terminology. I. Hubbard, Margie, date.
II. Title.
GV965.V29 1992   91-47579 CIP
796.352—dc20

Cover design by Mike McIver
Typography by Imagination Graphics

Printed in the United States of America
1 2 3 4 5 6 7 8 9 10

This book is printed on acid-free paper.
∞

We dedicate this book to our husbands who—
encourage us
listen to us
support us
love us and—
play golf.

ACKNOWLEDGMENTS

Our husbands, John Valentine and Mart Hubbard.

Cartoons - Ben Boyd
Title - Paul Marx / Harold Tabor
A special thanks to Bob Lovejoy, our head professional at Big Canyon Country Club, who helped us and encouraged us from the beginning.
U.S.G.A., Golf Digest, Fore, Dick McDaniel, Jo Valentine, Imagination Graphics, Gwen Williams, Terry Janes, Big Canyon Country Club, American Mailing (Bobbi Jacobs), Matt Mew, *Action On the First Tee* by Doug Sanders, Richard Boyle, Gordon Bagne, Charlotte and Judy at Charlotte's Word Processing, Arralee Hays, the Crest Printers, and Susan Dickman.
We would also like to thank the following golf clubs for contributing games that are played at their clubs:

Country Club of Peoria, Peoria Heights, IL
Rockford Country Club, Rockford, IL
Macktown Golf Club, Rockford, IL
Forest Hills Country Club, Rockford, IL
Ingesoll Golf Club, Rockford, IL
Sinnissippe Golf Club, Rockford, IL
Hinsdale Golf Club, Clarendon Hills, IL
Indian Hill Club, Winnetka, IL
Mission Hills Club, Northbrook, IL
Minnewaska Golf Club, Glenwood, MN
South Hills Country Club, Fon Du Lac, WI
Brown Deer Golf Club, Milwaukee, WI
Quit-Qui-OC Golf Club, Elkhart Lake, WI
Lake Creek Country Club, Storm Lake, IA
Storm Lake Club, Storm Lake, IA
Christiana Creek, Elks Country Club, Elkhart, IN
Elks Blue River Country Club, Shelbyville, IN
Pine Ridge Country Club, Wickliffe, OH
Pleasant Valley Golf Course, Payne, OH
Little Turtle Country Club, Westerville, OH
Cherokee Country Club, Knoxville, TN

Village Green Country Club, Bradenton, FL
Bent Pines Golf Club, Vero Beach, FL
Statesville Country Club, Statesville, NC
Willow Oaks Country Club, Richmond, VA
Country Club of Virginia, Richmond, VA
Centre Hills Country Club, State College, PA
St. Clair Country Club, Pittsburgh, PA
Livingston Club, Geneseo, NY
Tarry Brae Golf Club, South Fallsburg, NY
Hampton Hills Golf and Country Club, Riverhead, NY
Lake Isle Country Club, Eastchester, NY
Pawtucket Country Club, Pawtucket, RI
Navy Marine Golf Club, Pearl Harbor, HI
Waikoloa Golf Club, Waikoloa, HI
Bakersfield Golf Club, Bakersfield, CA
Tammarisk Country Club, Rancho Mirage, CA
Mt. Whitney Golf Club, Lone Pine, CA
Mesa Verde Country Club, Costa Mesa, CA
Marine Memorial Golf Course, Camp Pendleton, CA
Big Canyon Country Club, Newport Beach, CA
Ironwood Country Club, Palm Desert, CA
Alta Vista Country Club, Placentia, CA
Pinecrest Golf Course, Idaho Falls, ID
Boronado Golf and Country Club, El Paso, TX
Columbia Country Club, Columbia, MO
Franklin Country Club, Washington, MO
Oak Hills Golf and Country Club, Ada, OK
Hanover Country Club, Hanover, NH
Dartmouth Athletics Mens Golf, Hanover, NH

CONTENTS

CHAPTER 1

GAMES

TERMINOLOGY

CHAPTER 3

BETTING

CHAPTER 4

RULES FOR SURVIVAL

INTRODUCTION

As new golfers, we were totally unaware of the "games" that can be played on the golf course. So, when asked if we would like to play for "a nickel a hole and ties carry over" (later, we learned that this is a form of skins), we agreed, with no real idea of what we were agreeing to do. We resolved to look up this game and others. To our amazement, we found that there was only scattered information. At that moment, the idea for this book was born. After considerable research and contacting more than 8,000 golf courses, we have put together a book that, we hope, will provide you with information and a humorous look at the "Games within the Game!"

Linda Valentine
and
Margie Hubbard

"Behold the golfer, he riseth up early in the morning and disturbeth the whole household. Mighty are his preparations. He goeth forth full of hope and when the day is spent, he returneth, and the truth is not in him."
Anny.

GAMES

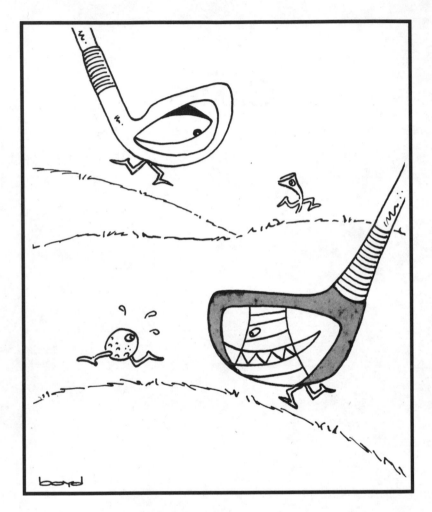

What kind of game is this?

CHAPTER 1

GAMES

In order to simplify your search for the game you'd like to play, we have grouped the games into twelve different categories. Many games fit into several areas so that you will frequently find the same game listed in several categories.

GAME TYPES

1. *INDIVIDUAL*
   Games where you want each player to have an individual score to win "the Game."
2. *PARTNERS*
   Games where you want two players to combine their score to win "the Game."
3. *9 HOLES OR TWILIGHT*
   Games which are suitable for abbreviated playing time and may be scored in a variety of ways.
4. *FOURSOME*
   Games suitable for playing and scoring as a group of four.
5. *18 HOLES OR MORE*
   Games that need to be played over 18 holes or more.
6. *THREESOME*
   Games suitable for three players.
7. *MIXED*
   Games suitable for men and women players as partners or individuals.
8. *MEN'S OR WOMEN'S*
   Games suitable to all men or all women players.
9. *BETTING*
   Games to bet on (you will probably find that you can bet on almost anything if you want to).
10. *MULTI-DAYS*
    Games that can be played over two or three days.
11. *CRAZY AND MISCELLANEOUS*
    No explanation needed here!
12. *PRO-AM*
    Games to be played with a professional's score as your partner's score.

GAMES	GAME TYPE
ACAPULCO	2, 4, 7, 8
ALTERNATE COUNTRY	11
APPROACH AND PUTTING CONTEST	11
BACKGAMMON GOLF	1, 3, 5, 8, 9
BACKWARDS	11
BAJA	2, 4, 7, 8
BALL BUSTER	1, 2, 5, 7, 8
BAND DAY	11
BEAT THE CHAMP	1
BEST OUT, BEST IN, BEST EIGHTEEN	1, 2, 4, 7, 8
BIDDING	1, 3, 4, 6, 7, 8, 9
BINGO BANGO BONGO	1, 2, 7, 8
BIRDIES OR BETTER	1, 2, 4, 7, 8
BISQUES (Also call BITS)	1
"BITS"	1, 2, 3, 5, 6, 8, 9
BLIND DRAW SCOTCH SCRAMBLE	3, 4, 5, 7, 8
BLIND NINE	1, 2, 4, 7, 8
BLIND PARTNERS	2, 4, 7, 8
BLUE BALL	2, 4, 5, 7, 8
BLUE GRASS SCRAMBLE	11
BONG	1, 2, 5, 6, 7, 8, 11
BRIDGE	3, 4, 6, 7, 8
BULLSEYE	4, 5, 6, 7, 8
BUNKERS	1, 11
BY THE PUTTER	1
CALLAWAY	1
CAPTAINS	2, 5
CASH	5, 8, 9, 10
CATS AND DOGS	1, 3, 4, 5, 6, 7, 8
CAYMEN - 9 HOLE	1, 2, 3, 4, 7, 8, 11
CHANGING PARTNERS	2, 4, 5, 7, 8
CHAPMAN	2, 3, 5, 7, 8
CHICAGO SYSTEM	1, 2, 4, 5, 7, 8, 9
CHIP-IN	1, 8
CHRISTMAS TREE	1, 8
CINCO	1, 2, 7, 8
CONSOLATION	1, 2, 4, 5, 7, 8
CRAZY SCRAMBLE	4, 5, 7, 8, 11
CRISS CROSS	1, 2, 4, 7, 8

GAMES	GAME TYPE
CROSS COUNTRY GOLF	1, 2, 4, 7, 8
DEFENDER	6, 8
DISC GOLF	11
DISTRACTION	1, 2, 7, 8, 11
DROP-OUT	1, 8
EIGHTEEN	1, 8, 9
ENGLISH BET	6, 8
EQUALIZER	1, 11
EVEN HOLES OR ODD HOLES	1, 2, 4, 7, 8
FIELD DAY	2, 4, 7, 8
FIELD SHOTS	1, 2, 4, 7, 8
FIFTEEN - TWENTY-FOUR - THIRTY-THREE	4, 7, 8
FLAG DAY	1, 8
FLORIDA SCRAMBLE	2, 3, 4, 5, 7, 8
FOUR BALL	2, 4, 5, 7, 8, 9
FOUR-MAN SCRAMBLE	4, 5, 7, 8
GET-ACQUAINTED	2, 4, 5, 7, 8, 9
GOAT	1, 5, 8, 13
GOOD, BAD, AND UGLY	1, 2, 4, 6, 7, 8
GREENIES	1
GROUND HOG DAY	11
HALLOWEEN	2, 3, 4, 7, 8
HANDICAP STROKE PLAY	1, 2, 4, 5, 7, 8, 9
HANGTIME	1, 2, 4, 8, 11
HATE 'EM	1, 2, 4, 7, 8
HAWK, THE	4, 9
HI-LO TOURNAMENT, THE NEW	2, 7, 8
HIT IT ALICE!	1
H.O.R.S.E.	1
HORSE RACE	2, 3, 7, 8
HORSESHOES	1, 7, 8
HUMILITY	1, 11
I CAN'T SEE IT	11
IF I'DA	1, 2, 4, 6, 7, 11
IRON PLAY	1, 2, 4, 6, 7, 8, 11
JUST ONE	2, 8, 11
KICKERS'	1, 2, 4, 5, 6, 7, 8
KING OF THE HILL	1, 2, 8

GAMES	GAME TYPE
LADDER PLAY	1, 5, 8
LAGGING	1
LAUDERDALE SCRAMBLE	4, 5, 7
LEAST PUTTS	1, 2, 4, 7, 8
LEGS	1, 5, 7, 8, 9
LET'S SEE IT AGAIN	1, 8
LONG AND SHORT	2, 3, 7, 8
LONG DRIVE	1
LOW BALL	1, 2, 6, 7, 8
LOW BALL - LOW TOTAL	1, 2, 5, 8
LOW NET PLUS PUTTS	1, 2, 6, 7, 8
MATCH vs. PAR	1, 2, 4, 7, 8
MATCHPLAY	1, 2, 7, 8
MATCH PLAY OFF LOW BALL	1, 2, 4, 5, 6
MEMBER & GUEST	4, 7, 8
MODIFIED COMBINED AGGREGATE	2, 5, 8
MODIFIED SCOTCH	2, 4, 7, 8
MONSTER DAY	1, 2, 3, 4, 7, 8, 11
MOONLIGHT MADNESS - ABCD MIXED SCRAMBLE	3, 7, 11
MOST THREE's, FOUR's AND FIVE's	1, 2, 4, 5, 6, 7, 8, 9
MULLIGANS AND HITAGAINS	3, 4, 5, 7, 8, 11
MUTT & JEFF	1, 2, 4, 7, 8
MY ONE AND ONLY	1, 2, 3, 4, 6, 8, 11
NASSAU	1, 2, 4, 7, 8
NICAROHDIES	1, 2, 3, 7, 8
NINES	1, 6, 8
NO ALIBI	1, 2, 5, 7, 8, 9
NUTSHELL CHAMPIONSHIP	1, 2, 5, 8, 10
ODD CLUB AND ODD STANCES ON EACH HOLE	11
ODD-EVEN	4, 7, 8
ONE AND A TWO	4, 7, 8
ONE CLUB SCRAMBLE	1, 2, 3, 4, 5, 6, 7, 8, 11
ONE-TWO-THREE	4, 7, 8
O-N-E-S	1, 2, 4, 7, 8
OUTSIDERS	1
OVERS	4, 5, 7, 8, 11
PAR FOR A PARTNER	2, 6, 8

GAMES	GAME TYPE
PAR FOURS	1, 2, 4, 7, 8
PARTNER'S BETTER BALL	2, 4, 7, 8
PARTNER'S ECLECTIC	2, 4, 7, 8
PARTNER'S ODD AND EVEN	2, 4, 7, 8
PECK'S BAD BALL	1, 6, 8
PEORIA HANDICAP SYSTEM	1, 2, 3, 4, 7, 8
PICK AND HIT	2, 3, 4, 5, 7, 8
PICK YOUR PRO PARTNER	2, 5, 9
PLAY IT AGAIN "SAM"	1, 8
PLAY WITH THE PROS	2, 12
PLUS AND MINUS POINT SYSTEM	1, 2, 4, 7, 8
POINTS FOR PUTTS	1, 2, 3, 4, 7, 8
POINT PAR	1, 2, 4, 7, 8
PRACTICE GREEN	1, 7, 8, 11
PRACTICE TIME OR TIRE GOLF	11
PRO vs. MEMBERS	1, 8, 13
QUOTA SYSTEM	1, 2, 4, 7, 8
RABBIT	1, 2, 3, 5, 6, 7, 8, 9, 11
RED BALL	2, 3, 4, 7, 8
RED, WHITE, BLUE SCRAMBLE	3, 4, 7, 8
REJECTS	1, 2, 7, 8
RENO PUTTS	1, 7, 8
REPLAY	1, 2, 5, 7, 8, 9
RINGER	1, 8, 13
ROLLING FOR DRINKS	11
ROUND-ROBIN	1, 4, 7, 8
ROUND-ROBIN BY POINTS	1, 4, 5, 8, 9
SANDIES	1, 5, 8, 9
SCOTCH	2, 3, 7, 8
SCRAMBLE	4, 7, 8
SCRAMBLE QUOTA	4, 7, 8
SCRAMBLES	4, 5, 7, 8
SCRATCH AND SCRAMBLE	2, 4, 7, 8
SELECTED SCORE - ECLECTIC	1, 2, 4, 5, 7, 8, 10
SELECTIVE NINE	1, 2, 4, 7, 8
SEVEN-UP	1, 8, 10
SHOOT-OUT	1, 5, 8, 9
SHOTGUN	1, 2, 4, 7, 8
SIC	1, 2, 7, 8, 11

GAMES	GAME TYPE
SIX AT A TIME	2, 4, 5, 7, 8
SIX FOR THREE	1, 5, 8, 9, 11
SIX-SIX-SIX	4, 7, 8
SKINS	1, 8
SKINS WITH CARRY OVERS	1, 5, 8, 9
SNAKE	1, 6, 7, 8
SPECKS	1, 2, 6, 7, 8
SPLASH	1, 3, 5, 8
SQUIRREL	1, 5, 8, 9
STABLEFORD	1, 5, 8, 10
STRING GAME	1, 2, 4, 7, 8
STYMIES	1, 7, 8, 11
SUCKER IN THE BUCKET	4, 5, 7, 8
SWEEPS TOURNAMENT, (see HI-LO)	2, 5, 7, 8, 9
SWING BET	1, 2, 5, 8, 9
SYNDICATE	1, 2, 8
T AND F	1, 2, 4, 7, 8
TEE FOR ALL	1, 5, 8, 11
TEE TO GREEN	1, 2, 4, 6, 7, 8, 11
THIRTEEN HOLES	3
THREE BETTER BALLS OF FOURSOME	4, 7, 8
THREE BLIND MICE	1, 2, 4, 7, 8
THREE CLUB MATCH	1, 2, 5, 7, 8, 11
THREE-TWO-ONE	4, 7, 8
TIJUANA	2, 4, 7, 8
TIN WHISTLE	1, 2, 4, 7, 8
TIRE GOLF	1, 2, 8, 11
TOP GUN	1, 6, 8
TOURNAMENT FUN	11
TWO AGAINST ONE	1, 7, 8, 11
TWO BETTER BALLS OF FOURSOME	4, 7, 8
TWO PLAY	2, 7, 8
U BET	1, 8, 11
UP AND DOWN	1, 8, 11
UPSIDE DOWN	11
VEGAS	2, 4, 5, 7, 8
WIN BY THE FOOT	1, 5, 8
WIN, PLACE, SHOW	1, 2, 3, 4, 6, 7, 8
WOLF	4, 5, 6, 7, 8, 9

GAMES

GAMES

ACAPULCO

Pick a partner and go for low score. Both partners drive from each tee and select one ball to play, alternating shots thereafter.

ALTERNATE COUNTRY

Select holes 1 or 10, 2 or 11, 3 or 12, etc. until you have 9 scores. Subtract one-half your handicap.

APPROACH AND PUTTING CONTEST

Each contestant approaches and putts out three balls from 25, 50 and 100 yards off the green. In each case, the ball should be played from a different direction. The winner is the one holing out the three balls in the fewest number of strokes.

BACKGAMMON GOLF

This is played against another player, hole by hole. Taking player A and player B, start with $1 a hole (or any designated amount). Use a betting cube, like backgammon. When the hole begins, the cube is in neutral possession. Either player can double the bet at any time. For example, player A doubles the $1 bet. The hole is then played for $2 and the cube is in the hands of the player accepting the double. If player B does not accept a double from player A, then player B loses the hole automatically. Let's say player A doubles after player B hits a poor shot. Player B accepts. He then puts the next shot on the green and then doubles back player A. The hole is now played for $4 if player A accepts. If Player A doesn't accept, he loses $2. If he does accept and hits a good shot, he can double back player B. Player B accepts, so the hole is now $8. B makes his putt and now doubles back Player A. Player A either loses $8 or putts for the $16 to tie for no loss. If he misses, he loses $16. This can be played with strokes where they fall on the card.

To Beaver - If player A doubles on the tee before teeing off, player B can Beaver him. That means he thinks player A made a bad double and so doubles him back but keeps the cube.

BACKWARDS

Play the golf course backwards.

BAJA

Choose partners and both drive from the tee. Play a second shot with the others' ball. After the second shots, choose one ball with which to complete the hole, alternating shots.

BALL BUSTER (Also called MONSTER DAY)

Tees and pin locations can be and usually are in ridiculous spots.

BAND DAY

Early on the 4th of July, have a man dressed as George Washington arrive on a horse. Abe Lincoln can be there too. Arrange for a band to be at the 1st tee playing patriotic music prior to the shotgun, and have refreshments available: Pastries, fresh fruit, cereal and milk, Bloody Marys, Rum Stones, and Screwdrivers. During the playing of the National Anthem, have a World War II plane fly down the #1 fairway.

Play a scramble with the pins in ridiculous positions and just laugh! Golf is supposed to be fun!

BEAT THE CHAMP

All players whose net scores are better than the net score of the Club Champion share equally in the sweeps money for the day.

BEST OUT, BEST IN, BEST EIGHTEEN

Contestants play three matches. The first nine holes is one, the second nine another, and the full 18 holes is the third. One prize per player. Score this with strokes where they fall.

BIDDING

The object of the game is to win the most number of points in either 9 or 18 holes. Before teeing off, players agree on the value of each point. To determine bidding rotation on each hole, a ball from each player is tossed up. Pick up each ball and write the player's name in that order on the card. The designated bidder on the first tee can either bid, or pass (as in the card game, bridge). If he does not pass he must declare the maximum number of strokes he will need to finish the hole. For example: he might bid a PAR. At this point, each player (in rotation) has three options:

1. Underbidding and become the new BIDDER.
2. Accepting THE BID. (He believes the chances of the bidder making his bid are probably good.)
3. DOUBLING THE BID Double point value. (He believes the chances of the bidder making his bid are very slim.)

After each player has exercised one of the three options, THE BIDDER now must accept the challenge of each player, or redouble any player that doubled him.

Point Value After Bidding could be:
    Option 1 - point value doubled
    Option 2 - point value even
    Option 3 - point value doubled and redoubled

Points are figured at the end of each hole. The next hole will have a new Bidder, as determined by the rotation on the score card.

BINGO BANGO BONGO

Three points are awarded on each hole. One point is for first on the green (Bingo). One point is for closest to the hole, after everyone is on the green (Bango). One point is for first in the hole (Bongo).

BIRDIES OR BETTER

All birdies or better will be paid. The value paid will be determined by dividing the total monies from entry fees by the number of holes birdied. The hole value (what each birdie or better on that hole is worth) is established by dividing the number of birdies or better on that hole by the value of the individual birdie. Example: If the individual birdie is worth $15 and 3 birdies are made on hole #5, then each of those birdies is worth $5, etc. To play for points, award 1 point for each birdie or better.

BISQUES or BITS

In this game, players are given strokes (Bisques) based on the difference in their handicaps. The catch here is that a "Bisque" can be used where the player wants, as long as the player uses only one per hole.

"BITS"

1. Use 80 percent of your handicap to establish the number of "Bits."
2. The high handicap player may elect to use any or all of his "bits" *after* the completion of a hole.
3. It becomes a strategy game - where shall he take his allotted "bits" or strokes?

BLIND DRAW SCOTCH SCRAMBLE

The field is split into two teams (A&B) based on handicaps, with two men and two women on each team. An A-team and a B-team are paired by a blind draw. Format: Both men drive from the tee and the best drive is chosen. Both women hit from there; they select the best ball, and the men hit. Continue until the ball is in the hole. If the men putt last, the women tee off and vice versa except on three pars. Awards are given on three pars for closest to the pin. Some are marked for men and some are marked for women.

BLIND NINE

A blind draw of nine holes is made and placed in an envelope. The first group in opens the envelope, and only those holes drawn are counted, less one-half handicap.

BLIND PARTNERS

This is an 18-hole stroke-play round with 90 percent handicaps. Players may play with anyone of their choice...but...partners are not drawn until the last group has teed off, so a player does not know his partner until the round is finished. The winner is the team with the lowest better-ball score.

Blind Partners

BLUE BALL

Four-man team, best 2 balls of the foursome. One ball with a blue stripe counts as one of the scores. Each person must play with the striped ball on an alternating 4-hole basis. If the ball is lost, the team automatically loses. Otherwise, the low ball total for the round wins.

BLUE GRASS SCRAMBLE

Each team consists of an A,B,C,D player based on handicaps. The A player plays from blue tees, B and C players play from white tees, and the D player plays from red tees. All players tee off from their designated teeing grounds, select the best two drives, and mark their positions. At this point, the team divides into two 2-man teams who finish each hole per the Scramble format. The owner of a designated tee shot may elect to partner up and play either ball selected. (The division of two 2-man teams may change every hole.) Continue for 18 holes. Score both balls using one-fourth total handicap of the team.

BONG

The highest total loses to the others in the group, or over the field. Bong employs the following scoring system.

BONG	ASSESSMENT
Whiff	4
Teeing Off in Front of Marker	1
Lost Ball	2
Out of Bounds	2
In Sand Trap	1
In The Water	1
Two Strokes in the Sand Trap	3
Three Strokes in the Sand Trap	5
Hitting One Trap to Another	2
Three Putt	2
Four Putt	3

BRIDGE

Flip on 1st tee to see who gets to make the 1st bid. Players who win the flip "BID" what they think their combined score will be on the hole. Opponents may (a) double [if they think the score bid can't be made], (b) bid that their combined score will be less, or (c) pass. Scoring: If score is less than or equal to bid, the bidders win $.25, or 1 point plus $.25, or 1 point for each stroke under the "bid". If doubled, it is $.50 or 2 points a stroke and redoubled is $1.00 or 4 points. "Bids" made have the honor of the 1st bid on the next hole. Strokes over the "bid" are computed the same way, except the honor of "bidding" first is lost.

BULLSEYE

Four-man teams using the best three balls with handicap. On each hole one member of the team uses a colored ball and the score MUST be used on that hole.

Prior to beginning the round the team may decide the rotational sequence for the colored ball. The sequence must include all players, and once the round has begun this sequence cannot be changed.

This game puts pressure on one team member on each hole because he knows that the score obtained with the colored ball MUST count and he therefore wants to do well for his team.

BUNKERS

Before teeing off on each hole, each player must select one bunker on the hole that he will play through before reaching the green. This is one game where everyone is the winner since each player's sand play will be greatly improved.

BY THE PUTTER

Mark the spot where your first putt comes to rest and measure a putter length back from your mark. Take your second putt from there. This will make your next putt about three feet longer.

CALLAWAY HANDICAP SYSTEM

(by Lionel F. Callaway, Golf Professional, Copyright 1957, All rights reserved)

Under the Callaway System, a player's handicap is determined after each round by deducting the scores of the worst individual holes during the first 16 from the gross score for 18 holes . The following table shows the number of "worst hole" scores a player may deduct, and the adjustment to be made, based on the gross score. For instance, if a gross score for 18 holes is 96, the player turns to the table and finds that he may deduct the total for the three worst holes scored on Holes 1 through 16 inclusive. If the player has a 9, an 8, and a 7, the handicap totals 24. From the total, further plus or minus adjustment is made according to the adjustment shown at the bottom of each column. For a gross score of 96, the adjustment requires a deduction of 2, resulting in a final handicap of 22. Thus 96 minus 22 handicap equals a net score of 74.

	Score					Deduct
..	..	70	71	72	scratch	-- no adjustment
73	74	75	..	..	½	worst hole and adjustment
76	77	78	79	80	1	worst hole and adjustment
81	82	83	84	85	1½	worst holes and adjustment
86	87	88	89	90	2	worst holes and adjustment
91	92	93	94	95	2½	worst holes and adjustment
96	97	98	99	100	3	worst holes and adjustment
101	102	103	104	105	3½	worst holes and adjustment
106	107	108	109	110	4	worst holes and adjustment
111	112	113	114	115	4½	worst holes and adjustment
116	117	118	119	120	5	worst holes and adjustment
121	122	123	124	125	5½	worst holes and adjustment
126	127	128	129	130	6	worst holes and adjustment

Maximum Handicap: 50

Adjustment

–2	–1	0	+1	+2	Add to or Deduct from Handicap

Notes: 1. No hole may be scored at more than twice its par.

2. Half strokes count as a whole.

3. The 17th and 18th holes are never deducted.

4. In case of ties,lowest handicap takes preference.

CAPTAINS

On each hole, one player is captain and chooses a partner *after* tee shots are hit. The Captain may also play alone against the other three. Fun...with partners always changing. With a handicap, use full handicap strokes.

CASH

After play, score cards are collected and hole by hole scoring is used. Players over the field are responsible for payoffs to the winners. Payoffs are as follows: Par $1. Birdies $2, Eagle $3. If a hole is tied there is no payoff.

A variation: Play "Cash" as a Skins Game with carry overs.

CATS AND DOGS

The single lowest score on a hole wins the CAT. Playing carry-overs are an option. But here comes the DOG.

The DOG is the same as the cat, except in reverse. The single highest score on the hole (the DOG) pays each of the other players. The value of the DOG is usually one-half the value of the CATS.

CAYMEN - 9 HOLE

Players play the designated 9 holes with a Jack Nicklaus' Caymen Ball. Using one club is a variation when the Caymen ball is in play.

CHANGING PARTNERS

Each player is paired with a different partner in their foursome during the round (18 holes). The scoring format is low gross and low net for the team. Partners change either three times (six holes with each partner) or six times (twice with each partner, three holes at a time).

A variation: Play without partners and when the round is finished, pick partners and figure scores accordingly.

CHAPMAN

A form of competition in which two players who are partners play for a time with two balls, then hole out with only one ball.

On a par-3 hole, both players tee off, then choose the ball with which they would like to finish the hole. If that ball is the ball player A teed off with, player B hits the ball next. Each player hits the ball alternately until the ball is holed out.

On a par-4, the same procedure is followed except the players exchange and hit the other's tee shot. Then players select the best ball and hit alternately until the ball is holed out.

On par-5 holes, the players exchange hitting the other's tee shot twice before making the decision as to which ball will be holed out with alternate shots.

This game may also be played using the same procedure that is used on 4 pars.

CHICAGO SYSTEM

Each player is given a quota based on his handicap. For example: a 1 handicap = 39, a 2 handicap = 38, etc. Then, only gross score counts and points are awarded as follows: Eagle = 8 points, Birdie = 4 points, Par = 2 points, Bogey = 1 point, and anything else = 0. This may be played as a four or two-person team, and the team quota is the total quotas given to each team member. The winner is the person or team whose score is the closest to or most exceeds the quota.

CHIP-IN

Each golfer pays $.25 or more to enter. If he chips in, he receives the pot. For a chip-in to be legal, the player must be off the green. If two or more players chip-in, the pot is divided evenly. The winner may be paid in cash or credit in the pro-shop.

CHRISTMAS TREE

This is a variation of Flag Tourney. Add 72 to your handicap. When you have used up that number of strokes, plant your

Christmas Tree. If your last stroke reaches the green, measure the distance from the hole with the flagstick. Record the distance on your Tree and plant it on the rear of the green.

CINCO

Five points are possible on each hole. The scoring is: 2 points for low score, 1 point for closest to the pin, 1 point for a natural birdie, and 1 point for a sandy par.

CONSOLATION

This is held at the end of the season on any basis desired. The only players eligible to compete, however, are those who have not won a tournament prize during the season. Some clubs give a prize to every player in the tournament.

CRAZY SCRAMBLE

The total handicap for each foursome must be no more than 71. Everyone hits from the white tees unless otherwise instructed. Each player in each foursome is given a number, (1-2-3-4) and each foursome has one die.

Holes

1and2... Each player tees off, then the number 1 player rolls the die. That number determines which ball is used for the second shot, regardless of its position. The other players hit their ball from this position and continue this format to hole out.

Hole 3... Only the number 4 tees off. Women may use the ladies tee box. Using this as the drive, continue the scramble to hole out.

Hole 4... Hit from the white tee box. Roll the die for the second ball. Continue the scramble to hole out.

Hole 5... Only number 1 tees off. Women use the ladies tee box. Using this for the drive, continue the scramble to hole out.

Hole 6... Use only a 9 iron on this hole, and use a putter on the green. Everyone tees off. Roll the die and continue the scramble to hole out.

(Continued on next page)

Hole

7 and 8... Everyone hits from the white tee box. Roll the die to determine the drive used and use scramble format to hole out.

Hole 9... Everyone tees off. Women use ladies tee box. Roll the die to determine the drive to be used and use the scramble format to hole out.

Hole 10...Only number 3 tees off. Women use ladies tee box. Using this ball for the drive, roll the die and continue the scramble to hole out.

Hole 11...Everyone tees off from the white tee box. Roll the die and continue the scramble to hole out.

Hole 12...Only number 2 tees off. Women use ladies tee box. Use this ball for the drive, roll the die and continue the scramble to hole out.

Hole 13...Everyone tees off from the white tee box. Roll the die to dermine the second ball. That player hits the second shot, then alternate hitting the ball according to number sequence to hole out.

Hole 14...Everyone tees off. Women use ladies tee box. Roll the die to determine the ball used for the second shot. Roll the die and continue the scramble to hole out.

Holes 15

and 16... Everyone tees off from white box. Roll the die to determine the ball used for the second shot. Roll the die and continue the scramble to hole out.

Hole 17...Roll the die to determine who tees off. That player must hit from the white tee box.

Hole 18...Everyone tees off. Women use ladies tee box. Use the best ball for the second shot. Roll the die and continue the scramble to hole out.

Scoring is low gross per team. These instructions can be adapted to suit the holes on your course.

CRISS CROSS

Choose the best score from hole #1 or #18, #2 or #17, etc. ending with 9 holes for your score. Subtract one-half your handicap.

Cross Country Golf

CROSS COUNTRY GOLF

Usually played in the fall. Usually 9 holes. Played from any point on the course to any green on the course, and can be played with one club for variation. Gross score only.

DEFENDER

This is for three players. The object is to win as many points as possible. Before teeing off, all golfers agree on the value of each point for betting purposes. To determine the Defender, each player tosses a golf ball. The two closest balls are partners against the Defender. To determine who will be the Defender next, simply toss the balls again. The ball closest to the player who was the first Defender is now his partner. Continue the same rotation for the entire 18 holes.

The Defender plays against the other two players. If the Defender has a 4 against the other players' 5, he wins 2 points and defends the hole. (1 point for each player) If he has a 6 he looses the hole and the other two players win a point apiece. Each player is the Defender on every third hole.

DISC GOLF

Played like golf but using a frisbee. One point for each time the disc is thrown and when a penalty is incurred. To complete a hole, a player must have his disc come to rest in the DISC POLE HOLE BASKET. The object is to acquire the lowest score. TEE THROWS: Tee throws must be completed within or behind the designated tee area. LIE: The spot where the throw lands. The player who is farthest from the hole always throws first, until the hole is completed. Then, the player with the least amount of throws on the previous hole tees off first on the next hole. FAIRWAY THROWS: Fairway throws must be made with the foot closest to the hole on the lie. The other foot may be no closer to the hole than the lie. After release, a run up and normal follow-through is allowed. DOG LEG: A dog leg is one or more designated trees or poles in the fairway that must be passed on the outside when the player is approaching the hole. Until the dog leg is passed, the closest foot to the dog leg must be on the lie when the disc is released. PUTT THROW: Within 10 yards of the disc pole hole basket, a player may not step past the point of his lie when trying to make his putt throw. Falling or jumping putts are not allowed. UNPLAYABLE LIE: Any disc that comes to rest more than 6 feet above the ground is considered an unplayable lie. After a player declares an unplayable lie, the disc must be thrown from the new lie, directly underneath the unplayable lie. (1 point throw penalty) OUT OF BOUNDS: A throw that lands out of bounds must be played at the point the disc left the playing field. Water hazards and public roads are always out of bounds. (1 point penalty.) COURSE COURTESY: Don't throw until the players ahead of you are out of range.

DISTRACTION

Use noise or distraction (other than physical) during a swing, per hole. This can occur anytime during play.

DROP-OUT

Each player plays against par. Using handicaps, players remain in the contest until they lose a hole to par. The player who goes the farthest wins.

EIGHTEEN

Played on the putting green. The object is to total 18 points exactly. Score 3 points for a one putt and 2 points for closest to the hole. If you exceed EIGHTEEN, you are penalized the amount for which you've gone over. (i.e. A player with 16 points sinks a putt for a total of 19 points. Eighteen minus 19 is −1, so now the player has 15 points).

Distraction

ENGLISH BET

This is a game for a threesome that awards six points on each hole with points divided in one of three ways:
1. Lowest score = 4 points
   Next to lowest = 2 points
   Next lowest = 0 points
2. Two players with
   lowest score = 3 points each
   Third person = 0 points
3. Lowest score = 4 points
   Two players with next lowest score = 1 point each

Player with the most points wins.

EQUALIZER

The player with the highest handicap has his own EQUALIZER. This advantage can be used in one of three ways:
1. One under handed toss per hole to be used anywhere.
2. One free drop on every shot to be used anywhere from tee to green, including in the hole on an arms length putt. The drop must be made with arm fully extended.
3. All shots may be improved by the length of one club anywhere, excluding the green.

EVEN HOLES OR ODD HOLES

Total of even numbered holes or odd numbered holes less one-half your handicap.

FIELD DAY

Each member brings three guests for the play, and usually for dinner. The play may be by teams of four, each member and his guests matching their best ball against that of the other groups, or it may be individual handicap stroke play. Additional prizes may be awarded for the best guest scores. The event is an excellent way to interest visitors in membership.

FIELD SHOTS

Count all strokes (including penalties) except those made on the putting surface. If any part of the ball is touching the putting surface, it is deemed "on". Subtract one-half handicap for your score.

FIFTEEN – TWENTY-FOUR – THIRTY-THREE

Score 1 best ball on 5 pars, 2 best balls on 4 pars, and 3 best balls on 3 pars. Score gross and net with strokes where they fall.

FLAG DAY

The player who carries his flag through the most holes wins. Every player receives a flag to place on the course when his score equals par plus his handicap. (i.e. If par equals 72, and the player has a handicap of 25, 97 strokes may be taken before the flag is placed, even if the player finishes 18 holes and must play one or two more holes).

FLORIDA SCRAMBLE

The FLORIDA SCRAMBLE is played the same as the SCRAMBLE with the exception of one rule. The player whose shot was selected must sit out for the next shot.

If player #1 was selected to have the best tee shot, player #1 cannot hit the second shot. But he will be able to hit the third shot. The player's shot that was selected to be the best second shot must sit out the next shot, etc. Upon reaching the putting surface, all players are eligible to putt.

FOUR BALL

Choose partners before teeing off. Golfers will use all four scores to determine the winning or losing of a hole. There are variations of Four Ball matches, such as:
1. The total scores of you and your partner matched against the scores of your opponents.
2. The low score and the total of both scores matched against the low score and total of your opponents' score.

FOUR-MAN SCRAMBLE

Each team consists of an A, B, C, and D player based on handicaps. A players play from blue tees, B and C players play from white tees, and D players play from red tees. After all players tee off from designated teeing rounds, select best tee shot and mark position. All players then play second shot from marked position and select best position again. Continue until ball is holed out.

GET-ACQUAINTED

Each player must select a partner, a player with whom they have never played. They play a stroke-play round as a team, the score usually based on their better ball, with gross and net prizes. Each team is paired with another so that play is in groups of four.

GOAT

Each member of the club is given an inexpensive token in the form of a goat, with his name on the reverse side. Any player may then challenge another to a handicap match, the winner to get the loser's "goat." After a player has lost his goat, he may continue to challenge in an attempt to get another player's goat. Should he lose however, and not have a goat with which to pay, he must purchase a "kid" for a nominal amount from the professional, and give up the kid. The kid can be exchanged for merchandise in the professional's shop. Only players with a goat in their possession may be challenged, and players usually are not required to accept a challenge more often than once a week. Records of goat play and the current location of each goat usually are posted so that a player may know who has his goat and who has the most goats. The winner is the player holding the most goats at the end of the season.

GOOD, BAD, AND UGLY

Points are structured to reward good shots and penalize bad ones. Bogies are 1 point, pars are 3, birdies are 6, and eagles are 9. Bad shots are penalized by subtracting 2 points for double bogies and 5 points for triple bogies. Highest score wins.

GREENIES

These are tee shots on par-3 holes won by the member of the group who hits his shot on the green and nearest to the hole, for 1 point. (Note: In some people's game the winner sacrifices his greenie if he three-putts the hole. In that case, the next player with the ball closest to the hole wins the greenie. If only one player hits the green but then three-putts, no greenie is awarded.)

GROUND HOG DAY

Each player must tee off once on each side with the ball on a styrofoam cup. Do this on holes marked on card by tournament chairman.

HALLOWEEN

Each player MUST wear a costume! All tees have real pumpkins for markers. Special scorecards are used and each hole has been named something to fit the occasion. The course is played in reverse order. Temporary tees are set up near the regular greens and temporary greens set on or near tees. This may work best when the Sunday nearest Oct. 31 marks the close of the season. At Dutcher Golf Club in Pawling, NY, they serve a buffet between nines, and parade through the town in golf carts after 18. Prizes are given for costumes. FUN!!!!! FUN!!!!! Score is partners or foursomes best ball.

HANDICAP STROKE PLAY

Players play 18 holes at stroke play. Prizes may be awarded for best gross and net scores. Full handicaps are used.

HANGTIME

With stop watch, time longest time in the air off the tee. Add the seconds for a winner per hole, or add after 18.

HATE 'EM

Before teeing off, circle two holes that you absolutely H A T E. Subtract the score on these 2 holes from your total!

HAWK

Use four players (A-B-C-D) of roughly equal ability, or give handicap strokes as they fall. Establish the HAWK, the betting unit per hole, and the hitting order. After tee shots, HAWK selects a partner or plays alone against the other players. The other players may double anytime. The HAWK can accept or surrender the original bet. The HAWK can double back and the other players can either accept the double back or surrender the doubled amount.

If the hole is tied, no money is lost. The 2nd hole is started with the last amount bet and Player B is the HAWK for the hole. Players repeat the procedure. You can play unlimited carryovers.

On par three holes, if the HAWK is going to play alone against the best ball of the other three, he must declare before another player's tee shot is hit. If he wins, he's paid by all three, but of course, he also risks losing three bets.

Mark scorecard after each hole to keep track of money standing. i.e., A + 12, B − 12, C − 12, D + 12. The scorecard usually looks something like this after 18 holes: A + 54, B + 37, C + 12, D + 40.

This format makes for a lot of fun as pressure changes hole by hole, shot by shot.

HI-LO TOURNAMENT

The Teams: The 120 participants are divided into "high" and "low" handicap groups of 60 each. Each team is formed by a blind draw of one player from each group, until 60 teams are formed.

The entire tournament is based on the better-ball score of each team, using 100% of the official handicaps.

This tournament is for prizes, glory, and honor. The main prizes are for 36-hole play, but there are also prizes for Friday play only and Saturday play only.

Hit it Alice!

HIT IT, ALICE!

In this game if a player's putt would have tied or won the hole but is left short, the player is penalized. The penalty is determined before teeing off on the first hole.

H.O.R.S.E.

Two players flip a coin to determine "honors" or first person to putt. The winning player can putt at any hole from any spot that he chooses. As long as he continues to make his putts, the second player must putt from the same proximity. Each time the second player misses, he adds a letter. Example: the first putt he misses, he is an H.; the second putt he misses he is an O., etc. Once the first player misses, the second player may now putt at any hole of his choosing. If he makes his putt while he is the leader, the first player must make his putt from the same spot, or add a letter to himself. The first player to spell H.O.R.S.E. loses.

HORSE RACE

Ten men with the lowest handicap and 10 women with the lowest handicaps meet on the 1st Tee. Players are paired by the pro with the lowest man to the highest women, etc. (i.e., 5 & 20, 7 & 19, etc.). One team is eliminated on each hole for nine holes. The last team is the winner.

HORSESHOES

Play this on the putting green with scoring just like horseshoes except that sinking the putt is like a "ringer" (3 points) and leaving the ball by the hole is like having the horseshoe closest to the stake (1 point). The first one to reach 21 points wins. If no one makes a "ringer" (sinks a putt), the closest to the hole gets 1 point. In a popular variation of the basic game, if Player A makes a putt (3 points) and Player B puts one in on top of his, Player B gets 6 points and Player A's 3 points are taken off. (That's the equivalent of "covering a ringer with a ringer of your own" in horseshoes.)

The player who's scored on the previous putt has the honor of going first on the next series. Play continues until one player reaches 21 points.

HUMILITY

As soon as you lose a hole, you have to carry your opponent's bag until you win a hole back.

I CAN'T SEE IT

Hit the ball once on each hole with a bag on your head.

IF I'DA

During the play of an 18-hole round a player may "replay" three unsatisfactory strokes and does not count these three in the score. Each time an "IF I'DA" is used, it must be announced to your playing companions (i.e., if an errant tee shot finds a lake, the player may announce "If I'da", re-tee and lie one). REMEMBER ONLY 3 allowed. No posting.

IRON PLAY

Hit a wood off the tee. All succeeding shots must be hit with an iron. Regular scoring.

JUST ONE

You and your partner pick one club each - for entire round of golf (i.e., one picks a 5 iron - the other a putter). You must only use these two clubs and you must hit your own club. Gross score only.

KICKERS'

The tournament committee draws a number, advising players that it is, for example, between 60 and 70. Players select their own handicaps without knowing the number drawn. The player whose net score equals, or is closest to, the number drawn is the winner. This is a good type of tournament to schedule when accurate handicap information for a large percentage of the players is not available.

KING OF THE HILL

Play against another person or partners. Team must make 3 pars in a row or better to be "King". Every hole that is parred or better is worth $1.00 or 1 point. As soon as a bogie or more is made, you are no longer "King." You must then make 3 more in a row to get back on.

LADDER PLAY

At the start of the season, the names of all players are listed in order according to handicaps. Players with the same handicap are listed alphabetically. A player may challenge any one of the three players immediately above him to an 18-hole match. If he wins, they exchange places. If he loses, he may not challenge again until he has defended his own position against a challenge.

LAGGING

Select several holes to play on the putting green. Players score by always using two putts per hole. The player who sinks a putt or uses three putts loses to the player who takes only two putts. This helps new golfers learn how to lag putt.

LAUDERDALE SCRAMBLE

Each player on the team hits a tee shot. The team selects the best one and each player hits his 2nd shot from that spot. This is repeated until the ball is holed. The ball may be placed one club-length either side of selected ball through the green, 6 inches when on putting green. The ball may be improved (that is, the lie of it) anywhere on the golf course.

LEAST PUTTS

Count only strokes made on the putting surface. No handicap.

LEGS

For 2, 3, 4, or 5 players. The object of the game is to get four legs on the Rabbit. Before teeing off of the first tee, all players agree on the value of the rabbit, for betting purposes. At the first tee, the rabbit is considered "RUNNING." This means no one has a leg on the RABBIT. To get a leg, you must have a LOWER score on a hole than anyone else in your group. You will keep one leg on the rabbit until another player has a lower score on a hole than anyone else. When that happens, you lose your leg on the rabbit and the rabbit is running again. A player must win a hole in order to get a leg on the rabbit again and anytime a player can earn four legs on the rabbit, he wins. After a rabbit has been won, begin a new rabbit game on the next hole.

9-Hole Example

Hole 1...Player A <u>wins</u> the hole and now has one leg on the rabbit.

Hole 2...No one player wins the hole. Player A still has one leg on the rabbit.

Hole 3...Player A wins the hole. He now has two legs on the rabbit.

Hole 4...No one player wins the hole. Player A still has two legs on the rabbit.

Hole 5...Player B wins the hole. Player B does not have a leg on the rabbit, because the rabbit must be running before a player can earn a leg (ONLY ONE PLAYER AT A TIME CAN HAVE A LEG ON THE RABBIT). But because Player B wins the hole, he takes one leg away from Player A. Player A now only has one leg on the rabbit.

Hole 6...Player A wins the hole and again has two legs.

Hole 7...Player A wins the hole and now has three legs on the rabbit.

Hole 8...Player A wins the hole. He now has four legs on the rabbit and wins the rabbit.

Hole 9...Player C wins the hole and has one leg on the new rabbit.

The rabbit game can be played for 18 holes or for each 9 holes. At the end of the game, if a player has any legs on the rabbit he wins.

LET'S SEE IT AGAIN

After any shot you hit, an opponent can say, "Let's see it again" and you must replay the shot, and play out that ball. The other ball is dead and the stroke on it does not count. Only one replay per hole. A replay can be requested after any shot; no request can be refused! Nassau bets and presses can apply to the score of each player. Only three replays per 18 holes.

LONG AND SHORT

One player hits the drives and long shots to the green; the partner hits the shorter approaches, chips, sand shots and putts. Players can choose their partners. This may require a bit of strategy. Use one-half of the combined handicaps for scoring.

LONG DRIVE

The player hitting the longest drive off the tee wins this game. The drive must stay in the fairway!

LOW BALL

In this game each hole is given a pre-determined value (i.e. 1 point per hole or a graded system, 1 point for easiest hole, 2 points for the next most difficult and 3 points for the most difficult hole). The player with the low ball on each hole wins the pre-determined points for that hole. If a hole is tied, no points are awarded. Player with the most points wins.

LOW BALL - LOW TOTAL

This is a team game played in a foursome with two teams. Scoring is as follows: The player with the lowest score on the hole wins one point for their team, the team with the lowest total wins one point for their team for a total of 2 points per hole. If the low scores are tied no points are given.

Low Net Plus Putts

LOW NET PLUS PUTTS

Keep score for each hole and keep track of all putts. At the end of play, subtract your handicap, then add your putts to the net score. Example: if it took each of you 5 strokes to hole out (including putts) and you 1-putted and your opponent 2-putted, you would have scored 5 + 1 for a 6, and your opponent would have scored 5 + 2 for a 7. Low score wins.

MATCH vs. PAR

Par is your opponent. Strokes as they fall, score [+] if net score is lower than par, [–] if more than par, and [0] if even. Winner is most up on par.

MATCH PLAY

A round of golf scored hole by hole (one point for each hole). The player with the most holes is the winner. Total score by strokes is not a factor. Use handicap scoring.

When playing partners, use the best score between partners against the best score between the two opponents.

MATCH PLAY OFF LOW BALL

Lowest handicap receives zero strokes. Next lowest handicap receives strokes equal to the difference. Example: a 20-handicap vs. a 30-handicap, the difference is 10, so the 30-handicapper receives 10 strokes. The strokes are received according to the handicap holes. In this case, the 30-handicapper receives his strokes on handicap holes 1 through 10, and one point is awarded for winning the hole. If there is a tie for winner, each receives one-half point.

MEMBER & GUEST

The best ball of one member and one guest is scored on each hole. Regular scoring with full handicaps.

Moonlight Madness

MODIFIED COMBINED AGGREGATE

This game combines the gross score of partners and the net score of partners.

Gross score is the combined *total* strokes of partners for 18 holes.

Net score is the combined *net* strokes of partners, "modified" so that no player has scored more than a double bogey on any one hole.

MODIFIED SCOTCH

All players tee off, and partners decide which ball they want to play. The player who did not use his tee shot hits the second shot. Afterwards, the partners alternate hitting the ball until the hole is finished. To score, average handicaps by adding the two together and dividing by two. Subtract this number from the gross.

MONSTER DAY (Also called BALL BUSTER)

Tees and pin locations can be and usually are in ridiculous spots.

MOONLIGHT MADNESS

1 club, 1 putter, 1 night light golf ball, and a flashlight. All play 6 holes from ladies' tee markers. Begin 30 minutes before dusk.

MOST THREES, FOURS AND FIVES

Players use full handicap, taking the strokes as they come on the card. Prizes are awarded to the players scoring the most net 3s, 4s and 5s.

MULLIGANS AND HITAGAINS

With two players of unequal ability, rather than stokes, the higher handicapper gets a set number of mulligans and hitagains. A mulligan is a second chance after messing up a shot. A hitagain is what he can tell his opponent when the opponent hits a shot that is hard to duplicate.

MUTT & JEFF

Total scores on 3 pars and 5 pars. Subtract one-half your handicap for your score.

MY ONE AND ONLY

Use a putter and your choice of one club for *all* shots. Best gross score wins.

NASSAU

Three points are involved; one point for the front nine, the second point for the back nine, and the third point for the 18. The low score with full handicap on the front nine wins, and the same on the back nine. The player who wins the most holes out of the 18 wins the Nassau. Use full handicaps with strokes where they fall.

NICAROHDIES

Players buy X number of chips before teeing off. The value of the chips may be established by the players, tournament committee, or the pro-shop. At the finish of each hole, chips are exchanged among players (3 chips for a birdie, 2 chips for par, 1 chip for bogey). If a player runs out of chips during the round, he may try to purchase some from another player. Cash in chips at end of round. Maximum number of chips is set by either the players, pro-shop, or the tournament committee.

NINES

Three players only. The object is to get as many points as possible. Before teeing off, all players agree on the value of each point for betting purposes. There is a distribution of 9 points on each hole.

If all three players have the same score on a hole, each player is awarded three points.

If two players tie for the low score on a hole, each of them receives four points, leaving only one point for the third player who had the higher score.

If all three players have a different score on the hole, the low score receives five points, the middle score receives three points and the high score receives one point.

Total the points at the end of each 9 holes for each player. If player's handicaps are unevenly matched, points can be spotted to the higher handicap players to help even out the game.
Scoring is as follows:

> Low score on the hole . . . . 5 points
> Second low score on the hole . . . . . 3 points
> Third low score on the hole . . . . . . 1 point

or,

> Tie for low score on the hole . . . . . . 4 points each
> Third low score on the hole . . . . . . 1 point

or,

> Low score on the hole . . . . 5 points
> Tie for second low score on the hole . 2 points each

The value of each point can be worth any pre-determined amount.

NO ALIBI

Instead of deducting his handicap at the end of the round, each player is allowed to replay during the round the number of shots equalling one-half his handicap. A stroke replayed must be used even if it is worse than the original; it cannot be replayed a second time.

NUTSHELL CHAMPIONSHIP

A nine-hole stroke-play qualifying round played early in morning. Qualifiers are divided into flights of eight. Match-play draw is based on qualifying scores as follows: 1 vs. 8; 4 vs. 5; 2 vs. 7; 3 vs. 6. First-round matches of nine holes are played late in the morning. Survivors meet in the second round after lunch. Finalists in each flight meet in the third round of nine holes in the late afternoon. The result is over 36 holes in a single day, an abbreviated equivalent of a weekend qualifying and knockout tournament. This event is sometimes called a "Miniature Championship" and is especially good for groups at conventions and meetings held at resorts when there is a limited time frame.

One Club Scramble

ODD CLUB AND ODD STANCES ON EACH HOLE

Every player must use the club at the Tee box (which has been predetermined for each hole) and stand in the designated place to hit the ball, (not necessarily the Tee box.) Use full handicap for scoring.

ODD-EVEN

Played in a foursome with two players scoring on the odd holes and two scoring on the even holes. To score, use one-half combined handicaps for the two playing the odd holes and deduct from the gross score on the odd holes, same scoring for the even holes. Total these two scores for the net score for 18 holes.

ONE AND A TWO

Each foursome plays with an orange ball. On each hole the orange ball scores, plus 2 of the other three balls. The team decides who is to play the orange ball on each hole. No player may play the orange ball on 2 consecutive holes.

ONE CLUB SCRAMBLE

You and your partners (playing as a foursome) each pick one club that you hit best with: one to drive with off the tee, one for the fairway, one for short shots and one putter. (Each player is responsible for hitting with the club he chose for each hole.) Team with the lowest gross score wins.

ONE-TWO-THREE

Score best ball on hole #1, 2 best balls on hole #2, 3 best balls on hole #3. Repeat cycle for 18 holes, or if it's easier to remember— score one best ball on holes 1,4,7,10,13, and 16; two best balls on holes 2,5,8,11,14, and 17; and three best balls on 3,6,9,12,15, and 18. You may use gross or net score for winners.

O-N-E-S

Total scores of holes beginning with the 4 letters O-N-E-S (1, 6, 7, 8, 9, 11, 16, 17, 18). Subtract one-half handicap for your score.

OUTSIDERS

This game is for those players who land on the green outside the length of the flag stick (approximately eight feet). The player who one putts from here wins a point from each of the other players. If the "outsider" two putts, no points are awarded. Should the player three putt, the other players win one point each.

OVERS

Anytime someone complains about a shot before the ball stops rolling, any other member of the group can call "overs", and the player *must* abandon the shot and hit over.

PAR FOR A PARTNER

In case you have an odd number of players use par or bogey for the odd player's partners score. Low handicappers will use par for a partner and high handicappers will use bogey for a partner.

PAR FOURS

Total all par fours and subtract one-half handicap for your score.

PARTNER'S BETTER BALL

Better score of partners on each hole is recorded. Gross and net.

PARTNER'S ECLECTIC

Two or more rounds. On the 1st day, the better ball of partner's is scored (gross and net). On the 2nd round, the team tries to lower the score on each hole. To arrive at the eclectic score, select the better score from rounds played for each hole.

PARTNER'S ODD AND EVEN

Before play begins, partners decide which partner's score will count on the even holes and which will count on the odd holes. Strokes where they fall. Record gross and net scores.

Pick Your Pro Partner

PECK'S BAD BALL

One golfer plays alone against the worst ball of the other two players. If the lone golfer has a five on a hole and the other two players have a five and a seven, the lone golfer wins by the score of five to seven. If the two opposing players have fours and the lone golfer has a five, he loses four to five.

PEORIA HANDICAP SYSTEM

The golf staff selects a par 3, 4, and 5 on each nine. Multiply the amount over par on the selected holes by 3 and this will equal the handicap to be deducted. Maximum score is double par. Example:

Player A   6 over par in selected 6 holes x 3 = 18 Handicap
Player B   7 over par in selected 6 holes x 3 = 21 Handicap

Player A	88 Scored	Player B	94 Scored
	–18 Handicap		–21 Handicap
	70 Net		73 Net

PICK AND HIT

On certain 3-par holes, the pro-shop or tournament committee puts out a number of different prizes. Each player picks the prize he wants to play for. If the ball is in the circle that is on the green, the prize is free. If the ball is on the green it is 50% off. If the player misses the green, he pays full retail price.

PICK YOUR PRO PARTNER

The member looks at the newspaper list of 36 hole qualifiers of the current week PGA event (those who made the cut), and picks a "partner." After playing his round, he turns in his card. His net score combined with his touring pro partner's round for that day comprises the team result. For instance, a scoreboard from a Saturday during the Masters looks like this:

Member - Norman   67-66 = 133
Member - Ballesteros 67-70 = 137

Entry fee is $2 - $5, and the whole "purse" is given back in gift certificates or cash. Pros may be partners to more than one member.

PLAY IT AGAIN "SAM"

Each golfer has the privilege of making his opponent replay any four shots during the 18 holes. These may be shots that are considered lucky or difficult to be repeated.

PLAY WITH THE PROS

In the final round of any of the major tournaments, the player's net score is added to the score of the pro of his choice. This gives the player a two-ball score, the lowest two balls being the winning score.

PLUS AND MINUS POINT SYSTEM

Net score only: Double bogey or more = –2, bogey = –1, par = 0, birdie = 2, and eagle = 4. The player with the most points wins.

POINTS FOR PUTTS

All players are allowed one putt on each hole. Scoring is as follows: 1) 1 point for closest to hole; 2) 2 points for closest <u>and</u> past the hole; 3) 3 points for making a 1 putt.

POINT PAR

Score one point for par, 2 for birdie, 3 for eagle. The player with the most points wins.

PRACTICE GREEN

An 18-hole event on the practice putting green. Winner is determined by total putts. In case of ties, all tying contestants play extra holes at "sudden death." If the club has no practice green, use the "clock" method on one of the regular greens near the clubhouse by marking off nine "tees" at varying distances around the edge of the green; each player putts from these nine tees to cup.

PRACTICE TIME (Also called TIRE GOLF)

Saves the expense of maintaining greens and fairways. Lay a car tire on each "green site." A player is deemed to have holed out in the number of strokes taken to hit the tire, . If a player can chip into the middle of the tire, and his ball remains inside the tire, then he has holed out with that stroke.

A number of advantages accrue from tire golf. Strategy as well as skill adds zest to the game. For example, does the player who lies 2 at the edge of the green site go for a "hit" and a safe par or does he risk pitching for an "in" and a birdie, knowing that if he overshoots he will have to chip in with his next stroke to save his par? Tire golf produces more dramatic finishes than regular putting.

The number of clubs is reduced and play is much quicker.

PRO vs. MEMBERS

The club professional agrees to play a handicap match against each member as he is challenged, making a nominal charge for each round. The professional plays from scratch. The member making the best showing in his match receives a prize from the professional at the end of the season.

QUOTA SYSTEM

Each player is given a point quota, based on handicap. In using the quota system, all scoring is based on Gross Scores. Record Gross Scores only. Points are scored as Bogey 1, Par 2, Birdie 3, Eagle 6, and Double Eagle/Hole in One 10. The number of points a player must obtain is decided by subtracting his handicap from 36 (maximum handicap, 28). After 1st round, each player's quota-points will be adjusted one-half, both up and down to arrive at the quota points needed for 2nd round. Team with most + points or least –points wins.

RABBIT

The idea of the game is to have the rabbit at the end of 9 and 18 holes. The rabbit is free when the game starts. An outright skin claims the rabbit. The rabbit stays with his owner until someone else gets an outright skin and then the rabbit is loose...Another outright skin will again claim the rabbit... Whoever has the rabbit at the end of 9 and 18 holes wins a predetermined amount. One variation is that "greenies" may also claim the rabbit. Another variation: if you have the rabbit and don't at least tie low ball, you lose the rabbit.

RED BALL

On the first tee, each player must select the holes for which they will use the red ball. Only the red ball's score counts for the team score. In a threesome, each player will use the red ball six times. In a foursome, two of the players will use the red ball on five holes and two of the players will use it on four holes. For a variation, if a team loses the red ball their score will not count, and they are disqualified. Scoring for a foursome can be red ball plus best ball of other three, or just red ball.

RED, WHITE, BLUE SCRAMBLE

Variation of Scramble. Teams are paired (A-B-C-D). The low handicap player uses blue tees, 2 middle handicaps use white tees, and the high handicap uses red tees. After tee shots, proceed as a regular scramble.

REJECTS

At the conclusion of play, each player is allowed to reject his three (or any designated number) worst holes. Handicaps usually are reduced in proportion to the number of holes which are rejected. The winner is the player with the lowest score for the holes finally selected.

RENO PUTTS

Tally all putts for each player. A player is allowed to three putt on two holes without a penalty. If a player exceeds the allowed number of three putts, he must add five points to his total number of putts. It is possible to win from some players while losing to others. The scores are calculated by the difference in each player's putts.

Reno Putts

REPLAY

This is a variation of the No Alibi Tournament. Instead of allowing a player to replay a given number of his worst strokes, an opponent is designated for each player, and the opponent is allowed to call a given number of the player's <u>best shots</u> and ask that they be replayed. Each competitor must exercise all his replay options. Use the replayed shot, instead of the original shot, when totaling the strokes for the hole.

RINGER

A player builds his total over the season by posting his lowest score on each hole. Scoring is on a gross basis, or net basis as determined by your club.

ROLLING FOR DRINKS

When you are in the 19th hole after your round of golf and are ready for a drink, try this dice game to determine who pays for the round.

You need five dice and a cup to play this poker-like game. Ones are wild and may be matched with any other dice. The best roll is five 6's, which beats five 5's, which beats five 4's and so on. Five of any number beats four of a kind, which beats three of a kind, etc.

The game starts with each player "flipping" a single die to determine who goes first. High man wins, and if two or more players flip the same high number, they flip again to establish who starts play.

The high man rolls all five dice. He may roll as many as three times, each time setting aside any matching dice or other "keepers" for his final "hand." He may not, however, start saving any dice until one of the die he rolls is a 1.

The first roller may elect to stand with his hand after one roll. If he does, all other players may roll only once. If he takes two or three rolls, each player receives the same number of tries.

(Continued on next page)

After all players roll, the one with the best hand is eliminated from the game and from buying a round of drinks. If two or more players tie with the best hand, all players in the game roll again to break the tie.

Play continues until only two players remain. Then they roll head to head, each taking up to three rolls to build a hand until one or the other wins two hands out of three. The loser pays.

Some clubs count five 1s as a winner over five 6s, five 5s, etc. You can also play the game with no wild dice.

ROUND-ROBIN

Played in foursomes. Partners change every six holes, so each player is engaged in three six-hole matches with each of the others in the foursome as a partner. Score with strokes where they fall.

ROUND-ROBIN BY POINTS

All players agree on the value of each point. The partners are selected as in ROUND-ROBIN. The only difference is, instead of just winning by holes, each team tries to accumulate the most points.

Team winning a hole	1 point
Team getting a birdie	1 point
Team getting a greenie (on the green and closest to the pin with the tee shot)	1 point
Team winning a press	1 point
Team winning a robin	1 point

SANDIES

Played out of any sand trap on any hole. Player must go from trap to hole in two shots (sometimes called "up and down"). This earns one point. Should the player "hole-out" from the trap, he may earn two points.

SCOTCH

One partner tees off on each hole. Players alternate shots until ball is holed out. Alternate shots continue for entire round. Net is determined by using one-half of combined handicap.

In a threesome or a foursome, during any stipulated round, the partners will play <u>alternate</u> shots from the tee and <u>alternately</u> during the play of each hole. Penalty strokes do not affect the order of play.

In Match Play, if a player plays when his partner should have played, his side loses the hole.

In Stroke Play, if the partners play one or more strokes in incorrect order, such strokes are cancelled and the side is penalized two strokes. A ball is then put in to play as near the spot from which the side first played in incorrect order. Do this before a stroke has been played from the next tee or, in the case of the last hole of the round, before the side has left the putting green. If this is not done, the side is disqualified.

Threesome: A match in which one plays against two, and each side plays one ball.

Foursome: A match in which two play against two, and each side plays one ball.

SCRAMBLE

Each player tees off on each hole. Team selects the best positioned ball. Ball's position is marked, and all four balls are played within one foot of this mark. (May be placed by hand.) Each subsequent shot is made in the same manner. On the green, all putts must be made from the exact spot of the ball selected. Total gross score minus one-fourth of combined handicap is your team score.

SCRAMBLE QUOTA

Each team consists of players with handicaps from 1 to 30+. For 18 holes, quota for team is determined by subtracting one-half of each player's handicap from 18, add these together, and divide by 4. This number is quota for the team (i.e., handicap total is 75 for the four players, of which they get one-half which is 37-1/2, then divide this by 4 which equals 9-1/2, subtract this from 18 number of holes to be played, giving this team a quota of 8.) Play is Scramble with 1 point for par, 2 for birdie and 4 points for an eagle.

SCRAMBLES

Handicapped by Tees
Handicap

0 - 10	Blue tees to tee off
11 - 20	White tees to tee off
21 - 30	Gold tees to tee off
31 & up	Red tees to tee off

Everyone's drive must be used at least **4** times. On a short par 3 during the Scrambles use a **Caymen Ball**. Most players cannot reach the green with a driver. This provides a lot of laughs.

SCRATCH AND SCRAMBLE

Four-ball stroke play. On each hole, the partners' scores are added and divided by four to obtain the team score. The full handicap for each player is used. Divide by two if playing twosome partners.

SELECTED SCORE - ECLECTIC

Each player plays 36 holes. From his two cards, he selects his best score on each hole. The winner is the player with the lowest total score for the selected 18 holes. Prizes can be awarded for gross, net or both. This event may be completed in a day or extended over a weekend.

SELECTIVE NINE

Choose nine holes before play that you will score best. Subtract one-half handicap to determine your score.

Shoot Out

SEVEN-UP

The object is to work up to the top 3 spots for prizes. You can only challenge 7 spots higher. Example: if 7th player on ladder challenges 1st player (match play) 7th wins, 1 drops to 7th, and 7 to 1, but if 7th loses he buys the other a golf ball or drink. Play for a year, and at the end of the year, the top 3 players win prizes.

SHOOT-OUT

Nineteen players are pre-qualified and assemble on the first tee. All nineteen players, in one group, play the first hole and the player with the highest score is eliminated. If there is a tie for the highest score, the players involved then have a "chip-off." After chipping, the player whose ball is farthest from the hole is eliminated. Play continues on each hole until the 18th has been completed. The survivor is the winner. If handicaps are to be used, strokes are taken as they come on the card.

SHOTGUN

Each team tees off at the same time. Teams start play using all 18 holes.

SIC

When playing an opponent who is on the green in regulation and you are not, you may hit his ball with your putter anywhere off the green except into a water hazard. The opponent must then chip up and putt out. All strokes count. With partners, only one ball from each team may be hit off the green.

SIX AT A TIME

For fun and no boredom, try this for your next tournament! This game can be played with twosomes or foursomes. Play six holes using one ball for each team, alternating shots from tee to green. To score this portion of the game, gross is as played and net is the combined handicaps divided by 2 if a twosome and 4 if a foursome, subtracted from gross. Play the next six holes using the best ball of the partners for your score. Play the last six holes using a scramble format, in which each team member hits. Select the best shot and have each player hit from there. Repeat this format from tee to green; this will result in one score for the team.

SIX FOR THREE

Most games cannot accommodate six players. This one, however, does. Each team consists of three players and plays for one or more of three points: 1 point for best ball, 1 point for two best balls and 1 point for three best balls.

SIX-SIX-SIX

1 best ball on the first 6 holes, 2 best balls on the next 6 holes, and 3 best balls on the last 6 holes. Score gross and net with strokes where they fall.

SKINS

Skins is a match-play tournament. The "skin" is a point given to the player with the low score on a hole. In case of a tie, the points are carried over to the next hole. There are two ways to determine the value of each skin:

1. Set the value of each skin before starting.
2. Have players contribute a set amount to a pool. Divide the number of skins won at the end of the day into the pool to determine the value of each skin.

SKINS WITH CARRY-OVERS

The players determine the value of each skin before starting. If a player does not win a hole with the lowest single score, that hole is carried over to the next hole. This procedure is followed until a player wins a hole with the single lowest score. The player winning the hole also wins each hole that has been carried over. It is possible for one player to win 18 holes by having the lowest single score on the 18th hole, provided the low score on each of the 17 holes was tied by at least two players. IF ONE TIES, ALL TIE.

SNAKE

The person who last three putts a green has the snake. The golfer with the snake at the end of nine and eighteen pays the other three golfers the wager. Variation: Each 3-putt is a point. Add points at end of the round. Most points also pay a wager.

SPECKS

This game may be played individually or as a team. Specks are awarded for the following on each hole: longest drive on the fairway, first on the green, closest on approach to the pin, one-putt greens, and lowest total for the hole. Winner is the person or team with the most specks.

SPLASH

Players must contribute one new golf ball for every one they hit into a water hazard. A player not turning in his card is fined three balls just on suspicion. The lowest net scores divide up the balls on a 60-30-10 basis.

SQUIRREL

For 2, 3, 4 or 5 players. The object is to get four legs on the squirrel. Before teeing off the first tee, all players agree on the value of a squirrel, for betting purposes.

At the first tee, the squirrel is considered loose. This means no one has a leg on the squirrel. To put a leg on the squirrel, you must have a birdie (if two players have a birdie on a hole, no one gets a leg). If another player gets a birdie before you, he takes off a leg, and the squirrel is loose. The next player who gets a birdie adds a leg to the loose squirrel (only one player can have a leg on the squirrel at a time). If the player who had possession of the squirrel before it was set loose had two or more legs on it and recaptures it with a birdie, he can add the lost leg and then have two or more legs on the squirrel. Legs can only be added to a loose squirrel. If one player adds all four legs to a squirrel, he wins the pre-determined value set and a new squirrel is set loose.

STABLEFORD

A tournament format for multiple days which eliminates players each day (paying winners each day.) Scoring is based on plus points for double eagle ($+8$), eagle ($+5$), birdie ($+3$), par (0), and minus points for bogey (-1), and double bogey (-3). Accumulative 18 hole scoring is not used.

String Game

STRING GAME

Each player is given a length of string of one foot per stroke (i.e., a player with a 16 handicap will have 16 feet of string). Players are allowed to advance the ball by hand to a more favorable spot or even into the hole, measuring the distance with the string and cutting off the length used with a small pair of scissors. When the string is used up, the players are on their own. Don't be too cautious; use up your string!

STYMIES

A strategy putting game. Players select the number of holes to be played on the practice green and the distance from which to putt. There are two objectives to this game. 1) The fewest number of putts. 2) Leaving your ball in a position to block your opponent's next putt, if you are unable to make your putt.

No ball may hit another ball. Penalties for hitting an opponent's ball results in the loss of the hole, plus a point to each of the other players. You must putt last on the next hole. Putting line up is determined by the ball placement on the previous hole; in the hole or closest to the hole putts first, etc.

SUCKER IN THE BUCKET

After all four players have putted out, choose one ball to score. Next hole after putting out, choose one ball of the remaining three to score. Next hole, one of the remaining two to score. Next hole, use the player's ball you have not already used (that's your sucker). Next hole, start over again. Your 17th and 18th hole played...any ball can be used, but not the same ball twice. Variation: count only the "sucker" balls.

SWEEPS TOURNAMENT, THE (HI-LO)

This tournament is for money, and you may choose to participate or simply observe the action. The scoring is still based on the better-ball score of each team, using full handicaps—as in the official tournament—BUT WITH AN IMPORTANT "TWIST." Here's the deal:

Each team will be sold at a fixed price of $100. Since the price is fixed, the only way to "bid" on a team is to accept a total handicap less than the "official total handicap" of that team in the Main Tournament. Here's an example:

Harry Hotshot (10) and Danny Dubber (25) have been drawn as a team and are being auctioned. The official total handicap of the team is 35 (10 + 25). The bidding begins. Bidder A offers "32"...meaning he is willing to give up 3 handicap strokes in order to own the team. Bidder B offers "30". Bidder C bids "27". Finally, Bidder X (Monty Martini) bids "21". The bidding stops... no one is willing to bid lower. Monty is now the proud owner of the Hotshot-Dubber team and has paid $100 plus a "premium" of + 14 — the official total handicap of 35 less his bid of 21. Now, let's say that the Hotshot...Dubber team turns in a better-ball score (using full handicaps, of course) in the Official Tournament 61-64...total of 125. Their score in the Sweeps Tournament would be 125 plus the "premium" paid of + 14, or 139. So the winners of the Official Tournament and the winners of the Sweeps generally are not the same team...although it is possible.

Each team member has the option of buying 25% of his own team by paying the owner $25 before tee-off time. Also, each team member may bid on his own team in open bidding.

On occasion, a player will fail to show up at tee-off time. In that event, that team is eliminated from the Sweeps Tournament, the owner is reimbursed his $100, and the pool is diminished by that amount. If, however, a replacement can be found in time, the "new" team is eligible to compete in the Official Tournament, but not in the Sweeps.

The Pool will be divided as follows:

Place	Percentage
1st Place	25%
2nd Place	17%
3rd Place	12%
4th Place	10%
5th-10th Place	5%

Daily 1st and 2nd Places 2% and 1%
Ties will share equally the appropriate places.

(Continued on next page)

There will be a buy-out pool for those who are interested. The distribution of the buy-out pool will be to the first ten places in the official event. The cost of the buy-out will be $40 per team.

ALL TRANSACTIONS ARE CASH (CHECKS ACCEPTED). Successful bidders must pay for their team(s) at the conclusion of the auction. Payoff will be at the conclusion of play.

SWING BET

For five players only. Two players on each team play "match play" competition for a specified number of holes. A ball from each player is tossed into the air. The two closest balls are partners against three other teams. Example:

Players 1 and 2 are the two closest balls. They are partners.
Players 1 and 2 vs. 3 and 4.
Players 1 and 2 vs. 4 and 5.
Players 1 and 2 vs. 3 and 5.

Players 1 and 2 have 3 matches going at the same time. All other players have two matches going at the same time. After completing the specified number of holes, follow the same procedure for the next match.

SYNDICATE

The field is divided into classes according to handicaps: Class A may be players with handicaps of 7 and under; Class B, 8 to 15; Class C, 16 to 24, etc. The player who makes the lowest score in his class on a hole wins a syndicate. Syndicates may be cumulative; in the event that one or more holes are tied, those syndicates go to the next player who wins a hole. Each player pays an entry fee of one golf ball; the total balls in each class are divided by 18 to determine the value of a single syndicate, and each player's prize is determined by the number of syndicates won.

T AND F

Count the total strokes on holes beginning with T and F (2,3,4, etc.). Subtract one-half handicap for score.

TEE FOR ALL

A player has the option of teeing up any ball any time from tee to green. New golfers and a few "old" golfers will love this.

TEE TO GREEN

Count only the strokes from tee to green, no putts.

THIRTEEN HOLES

On a 9 hole course when some golfers find that 18 holes is too long and tiring and 9 is not enough, play 13 holes and enjoy.

THREE BETTER BALLS OF FOURSOME

Select 3 best balls on each hole. Gross and net scores may be kept, taking strokes where they fall for net score.

THREE BLIND MICE

Deduct 3 worst holes from score.

THREE CLUB MATCH

Usually played in a tournament and can be played as match or medal play. You can take only three clubs with you for the entire 18 holes. They can be any three clubs of your choice. Use full handicap for scoring.

THREE-TWO-ONE

Score 3 best balls, starting with the first hole, 2 best balls on the second hole and 1 best ball on the third hole. Repeat the cycle for the rest of the holes.

TIJUANA

The official play is for partners to alternate driving from each tee and then play alternate shots until the ball is holed. Lowest gross score wins.

Top Gun

TIN WHISTLE

Strokes as they fall, score 1 point for bogie, 2 points for par, 3 points for birdie, 4 points for eagle. Player with the most points wins.

TIRE GOLF (Also called PRACTICE TIME)

(See Practice Time)

TOP GUN

Players select a TOP GUN for 18 holes. On the first hole the TOP GUN plays one of the two players. If TOP GUN wins the hole, he receives a point and changes opponents. If he loses or ties, the TOP GUN keeps the same opponent until a hole is won. The third player gets points for picking the correct winner or loser or calling a tie, until it is his turn to play with the TOP GUN.

TOURNAMENT FUN

1) There are two holes on specified greens or each green. A player may hit to either hole. 2) No pin markers on any greens.

TWO AGAINST ONE

Use two putts to one putt to even up the putting game, if one player has putting abilities inferior to another player. (MY TWO AGAINST YOUR ONE). Use the difference in your handicaps to determine the number of holes in which 2 putts are allowed.

TWO BETTER BALLS OF FOURSOME

Select two best balls on each hole. Gross and net scores may be kept, taking strokes where they fall for net score.

TWO PLAY

Partners game - Five ways to score:
    1 point for first on the green (greenie)
    1 point for a birdie
    1 point for winning the hole by stroke play
    1 point for winning the hole by match play
    1 point for 1 putt

U BET

Using a player's net score on each hole, come up with the best poker hand over the course of eighteen holes.

UP AND DOWN

In this game a player who reaches the green in regulation is penalized by loss of the hole. The object is to place the ball near the green and use one shot to reach the green and one shot to sink the putt.

UPSIDE DOWN

Play across the golf course to different holes, using tee boxes that do not correspond to their holes.

VEGAS

Scores of all players are used on each hole, which keeps every player involved. This game is scored as follows: the low score (ball) for each team is put first. If a team makes a birdie, the other team must reverse its score. If both teams have a birdie, both scores are reversed and the difference in scores awarded to the team with the lowest score. If a player shoots 10 or more, that team's score is automatically reversed.

For example: on a four par, team A has a 4 and 5 for a score of 45. Team B has a 4 and a 6 for a 46. Team A gets 1 point (the difference between the scores).

Birdie example: on a par 5, one team has a 4 and 5 (45), and the other has a 5 and 7 (which becomes a 75), giving the birdie team 30 points.

WIN BY THE FOOT

The longest one putt on each green is awarded a pre-determined amount per foot.

WIN, PLACE, SHOW

Golfers play with full handicap. The low score wins three points, the second lowest wins two points, and the third lowest wins one point. The player with the most points at the end of 18 is the winner. A variation for a foursome: use points 4-3-2-1. Ties are allotted the same score.

WOLF

One player becomes wolf picked by lot on the first tee, and "wolf" then changes on successive holes through number 16. Every player (in a foursome) gets to be "wolf" 4 times. The wolf may pick a partner on any hole after tee shots are hit, or may decide he can beat the other three by himself. In this case he becomes a "Lone Wolf." Points are tabulated for all players after each hole. Full handicap can be used. The Wolf always tees off first. Ties carry over.

Variations:
1. AUTO-WOLF . . . Every "alternating" time a player is WOLF, he is a "LONE WOLF".
2. ONE LITTLE PIG . . . Bets are doubled. The WOLF'S partner is the PIG, who has the option of playing all other players alone. This means the WOLF also ends up playing <u>with</u> those who were not chosen as partners.
3. WOLF AND PARTNER . . . The WOLF must choose or pass a partner immediately after that player hits the ball, and before the next player tees off.
4. BLIND WOLF . . . The decision for the WOLF is to go "alone" or to pick a partner before any of the other players tee off.

WORST BALL SCRAMBLE

Play the worst shot of a foursome (or twosome if playing partners) until holed out. To score, add handicaps of the players and divide by the number of players. Subtract that number from the gross strokes for the score of the partners.

X-CEPT EIGHTEEN (18)

One best ball of the foursome on the front nine, two best balls on holes 10 through 17, and three best balls on the 18th hole.

XTRA TIME

If the pace is slow and you are a twosome, try this. On the first tee, Player A tees off and has the option of hitting a second drive if he thinks he can improve on the first. Then he can play the better of the two drives. Player B can hit the same number of shots as Player A. Once off the tee, regular rules are followed to determine who plays first. The player who hits first has the option of playing a second ball and always controls the number of mulligans. If his first shot is good, pressure is put on the opponent to make his first attempt a good one. When both players are on the green, the player farthest from the hole has the option of taking two putts. If Player A is on the green and Player B is not, Player B may opt to hit two shots to get on the green. This, however, allows Player A to take two putts if he is first to putt.

Handicapping for this game is figured at 75 percent of the difference in handicaps, divided by two. For example, if Player A has a handicap of 12 and Player B is a 4-handicapper, the handicap difference is figured as follows: Twelve minus four equals eight, 75 percent of eight equals six, and six divided by two equals three. Player A thus receives three strokes for 18 holes.

YARDAGE

In this game, when a player wins a hole he is credited with a number equal to the yardage of the hole. The player with the most yardage wins.

YIKES!

To play this round of golf, you and your partner each pick your favorite club. With only two clubs to play with, alternate shots (i.e., you may be chipping with a 5 iron). This format increases your expertise with your favorite club.

YOUR BALL

After teeing off, partners select the player who will hit the next shot on each ball. This is not on an alternating shot basis but on who will hit the next shot better. Both balls are played out. This game is scored with low ball and low total so each ball counts. This game may also be played as a foursome. Gross score only.

ZEEEE BEST

Each entrant plays every other entrant at handicap match play during the season; allow the full difference between handicaps in each match. A time limit usually is set for completion of each round: A player who cannot meet an opponent within the time limit forfeits the match but may continue in the tournament. The winner is the player winning most matches.

TERMINOLOGY

That's not the term I'd use!

CHAPTER 2

TERMINOLOGY

ACCELERATION/TO ACCELERATE

The speed of your down swing as you hit the ball—also, a ball that is hit will accelerate or seem to "take off."

ADDRESS

When the golfer is in the correct position, ready to hit the ball.

ADJUSTMENT/TO ADJUST

A designated number of strokes are used on each hole according to an individual's handicap. When a player exceeds this number, the score is adjusted to the maximum number allowed.

ADJUSTED GROSS SCORE

A player's gross score minus any adjustment under Equitable Stroke Control. Used for handicap purposes only.

AERATE

A process of pulling out round cylinders of grass and soil from the fairways and green to supply the turf with air.

AGGREGATE

The combined total scores...of a tournament, which lasts more than one day.

APPEARANCE

(See Honors)

The privilege of teeing off first, after the first hole, because the golfer has the lowest score on the previous hole.

APRON

The grassy area surrounding the putting green. This grass is frequently cut shorter than the fairway.

ARNIE (awful)

An award given to a golfer who misses the fairway on the tee shot but reaches the green in regulation and putts out in par or better. This is named for Arnold Palmer.

AUTOMATIC PRESS

When presses are made without having to communicate them to your opponent. The Automatic Press is the same as the Press, except a player DOES NOT have a choice as to when he adds a press. The Press is automatically added anytime a player is two down on any bet.

AWAY SHEET

The document used for posting your scores when playing a golf course other than your own.

BACK

The position of the golf ball in relation to a golfer's right foot (a left-handed golfer's left foot), or the position of the golf ball on the putting green.

BALL MARK

The mark left by the golf ball landing on the green.

BALL RETRIEVER

An instrument used to extract golf balls from the water.

BARKIE

When a player has hit a tree and still makes par, he has made a "barkie."

BEST BALL

A match in which a golfer plays against the best ball of other players in the group.

BETTER BALL

The lowest net score of one ball per team on each hole is used for scoring purposes.

BIRD

Finishing a hole one stroke under par.

BIRDIES

Multiple holes finished one stroke under par.

BLADE

The edge of the iron clubhead that makes contact with the golf ball (clubhead blade).

BLIND DRAW

The process of pairing up players by selecting the names from a "hat."

BOGEY

Finishing a hole one stroke over par.

BREAK

The contour of the putting green that causes the ball to change direction or to move or "break" one way or the other.

BUNKER

A sand or grass pit along the fairway or around the green, used to increase the difficulty of play.

CALCUTTA

A format for tournament play. Players are paired (normally by a blind draw) and auctioned off to the highest bidder. After play is complete, the funds collected are dispersed according to the final scores.

CALLAWAY HANDICAP SYSTEM

(by Lionel F. Callaway, Golf Professional, Copyright 1957, All rights reserved)

Under the Callaway System, a player's handicap is determined after each round by deducting the scores of the worst individual holes during the first 16 holes from his gross score for 18 holes. The following table shows the number of "worst hole" scores he may deduct and the adjustments to be made, based on his gross score.

For instance, if his gross score for 18 holes is 96, he turns to the table and finds that he may deduct the total for his three worst holes scored on Holes 1 through 16 inclusive. Therefore, if he has a 9, an 8, and a 7, his handicap totals 24. From his total, further plus or minus adjustment is made according to the adjustment shown at the bottom of each column. For a gross score of 96, the adjustment requires a deduction of 2, resulting in a final handicap of 22. So, 96 minus 22 handicap equals a net score of 74.

		Score				Deduct
..	..	70	71	72	scratch	-- no adjustment
73	74	75	..	..	½	worst hole and adjustment
76	77	78	79	80	1	worst hole and adjustment
81	82	83	84	85	1½	worst holes and adjustment
86	87	88	89	90	2	worst holes and adjustment
91	92	93	94	95	2½	worst holes and adjustment
96	97	98	99	100	3	worst holes and adjustment
101	102	103	104	105	3½	worst holes and adjustment
106	107	108	109	110	4	worst holes and adjustment
111	112	113	114	115	4½	worst holes and adjustment
116	117	118	119	120	5	worst holes and adjustment
121	122	123	124	125	5½	worst holes and adjustment
126	127	128	129	130	6	worst holes and adjustment

Maximum Handicap: 50

					Adjustment
–2	–1	0	+1	+2	Add to or Deduct from Handicap

1. No hole may be scored at more than twice its par.
2. Half strokes count as whole.
3. The 17th and 18th holes are never deducted.
4. In case of ties, lowest handicap takes preference.

CARRY OVER

A bet that is carried over from one hole to the other.

CASUAL WATER

A wet area on the golf course resulting in the golfer standing in water. The ball can be picked up and moved.

CELLOPHANE BRIDGE

An expression used when it seems as if the golf ball rolled over the cup without dropping into the hole.

CHAPMAN SYSTEM

A form of competition in which two players play with two balls, then hole out with only one ball.

CHI-CHI

When a player misses the fairway and the putting green and still makes par or better on the hole, he has made a Chi-Chi. This is named for Chi-Chi Rodriguez.

CHIP

A short shot from just off the green. Can be hit with a 6 iron to a sand wedge. The ball is hit with enough loft to carry onto the green, then roll to the hole.

CHIP AND RUN

Same as a chip shot. The intent is to roll the ball to the hole after it has landed on the green.

CHIP IN

To hit the ball into the cup from off the green with a short shot or "chip shot."

CHIP OFF

A method used to determine the winner of a hole. The closest chip to the pin is the winner.

CLUB

The instrument that is used to strike the ball.

COLLAR

The grassy area directly adjacent to the putting green, often a shorter grass than the fairway.

COMPRESSION

The amount of force needed to cause a ball to be compressed.

CUT

A shot that moves from left to right. Also, a term used to indicate a "cut" on a golf ball where the club has cut through the cover.

DIMPLES

The small indentations on a golf ball.

DIVOT

The depression in the grass or ground that is caused by the force of the golf club hitting or digging it up.

DOG LEG

A term used to designate the direction, either right or left, that the fairway turns.

DOUBLE BOGEY

Finishing a hole two strokes over par.

DOWN HILL

The lie or position of the golf ball when it is below the golfer's feet.

DRAW

A ball that goes straight with a slight right to left move or "draw" at the end.

DRESSING THE GREEN

The process of placing a layer of sand and organic material on a green to smooth the surface.

DRIVE

A term used to describe the first shot from the tee box on any hole.

DUFFED/DUFFING

Hitting the ball incorrectly.

DUFFER

A golfer who hits the ball incorrectly.

EAGLE

Finishing a hole two strokes under par.

ECLECTIC

A system of scoring that takes the best score for each hole from multiple days of play.

EQUITABLE STROKE CONTROL

"ESC" is the downward adjustment for handicap purposes of unusually high scores on individual holes under a prescribed formula.

EXTENDED PLAY

When play continues at a later time, usually the result of bad weather.

FACE

The area on the clubhead that faces and strikes the ball.

FADE

A ball, after it's hit, that moves off its straight line, veering to the right (left for a left-hander).

FAIRWAY

The short grassy playing area from the tee to the putting green.

FLAG

The marker used to indicate the position of the cup on the green.

FLAGGING IT

Hitting the ball to the green on line with the pole.

FRIED EGG

A golf ball imbedded in a sand trap.

FRINGE

The grassy area directly adjacent to the putting green, often a shorter grass than the fairway.

FRONT

The position of the golf ball in relation to a golfer's left foot (a left-handed golfer's right foot), or the position of the golf ball on the putting green.

GIMME

A golf ball which is so close to the hole that your opponent does not require you to putt it.

GINSBURG

The option on the tee to hit a second ball. On exercising this option, the player may choose to play the better of the two balls.

GINTY

A specialty club used most often for hitting a golf ball out of tall grass or other trouble spots.

GREEN

The playing surface where the flag and cup are placed.

GREENIES

An award given to a player who lands on the green and is closest to the hole on a three par, from the tee shot. In some people's game, if a player three putts he loses his greenie. If only one player lands on the green and three putts, no greenie is awarded for the hole.

GRIP

The rubber/leather sleeve that covers the end of the golf club. This term is also used to assess the manner in which you hold the club.

GROSS

The total number of strokes on a hole or 18 holes.

HAM AND EGG

When a team of two or more players scores well, while not playing well as individuals.

HANDICAP

The rating used to measure each golfer's playing ability.

HANDICAP SHEET

A computer printout with a golfer's handicap listed for the month, accompanied by a breakdown of his scores.

HANDICAP SYSTEM

1. Essence of USGA System

Handicapping, based on Course Rating, is the great equalizer among golfers of differing abilities. The national system of handicapping must meet two main requirements:

a. Simple enough for operation by the small, modestly-equipped club as well as the large club.

b. Thorough enough to produce fair, uniform handicapping the country over.

The United States Golf Association presents its Golf Handicap System, which uses the best 10 scores out of the player's last 20 rounds compared with the USGA Course Rating, in the conviction that, when faithfully operated, it results in equitable handicaps no matter where golfers live and play.

The System is based on the assumption that every player will endeavor to make the best score he can at each hole in every round he plays and that he will report every eligible round for handicap purposes, regardless of where the round is played.

It is a requirement of the USGA Handicap System that each golf club or golf association have a designated Handicap Committee which will maintain the integrity of the USGA Handicaps issued by the club or association.

2. Handicap Name and Certification Requirements

The terms "USGA Handicap," "USGA System," and "USGA Handicap System" are trademarks and service marks of the United States Golf Association.

Only a golf club or golf association (see Section 2) which computes and maintains a handicap in accordance with the USGA Handicap System as described herein may term the handicap so computed and maintained as a USGA Handicap and identify it on a card or elsewhere as a "USGA Handicap."

A golf association computing USGA Handicaps for its member clubs must obtain written authorization from the USGA.

If a golf club or golf association does not follow all the procedures of the USGA Handicap System, it loses its right to refer to any handicap as a "USGA Handicap" or to a handicap authorized or approved by the USGA and loses any right to use any part of the System, including the USGA Handicap Formula and the assigned USGA Course Rating, for any purpose.

3. Purposes

Among the purposes of the USGA System are to:

a. Provide fair handicaps for all players, regardless of ability.
b. Reflect the player's potential ability as well as his recent scoring trends.
c. Automatically adjust a player's handicap down or up as his game changes, while providing a period of stability.
d. Disregard freak high scores that bear little relation to the player's normal ability.
e. Make it difficult for the player to obtain an unfairly large handicap increase at any revision period.
f. Make a handicap continuous from one playing season or year to the next.
g. Establish handicaps useful for all golf, from championship eligibility to informal games.
h. Make handicap work as easy as possible for the Handicap Committee.

4. Championship Eligibility

Handicaps required of entrants for USGA Championships must be USGA Handicaps.

It is recommended that USGA Handicaps be required for eligibility for events of other golf associations.

Handicapping The Unhandicapped: The person who never plays except during a vacation or an annual tournament wants a fair chance in the competition for net prizes. A standard way of solving such a matter is to conduct a kicker's tournament. Each player selects their own handicap and then shoots at a score which has been drawn blind.

HAZARD

A grass or sand bunker or water hazard—used to increase the difficulty of play.

HEAD

The end of the club that strikes the ball is called the head or clubhead. These are different weights and slopes and may be metal or wood.

HIGH-LOW (HI-LO)

The pairing of two players in a tournament, one with a high handicap and one with a low handicap.

HOGAN

The definition given to a player who lands on the fairway, hits the green in regulation and putts to make a par or better on the hole. This is named for Ben Hogan.

HOLE IN ONE

Finishing a hole using only one stroke.

HOLED

A term that describes the condition of a ball that has been hit into the hole.

HONORS

The courtesy by which the player with the lowest score on the previous hole is allowed to tee off first on the subsequent hole. Continue until another player is the lowest scorer on a hole.

HOOK

A golf ball that goes severely to the left (right if a left handed golfer) when hit.

HOOKER

A golfer who consistently hits a ball severely to the left (right if a left-handed golfer).

HORSERACE

A golf game with multiple players (usually 20, two people per team), all teeing off on the same hole, and eliminating one team on each hole for nine holes.

HOZEL

The point on the golf club where the club head and the shaft meet.

IN THE LEATHER

A term of measurement used to designate a golf ball that lies between the hole and where the grip ends and the metal shaft begins.

IN YOUR POCKET

This is a term sometimes used when a player has picked up the ball before "putting out", usually because the maximum number of strokes have been used or the last putt was given to the player.

INDIVIDUAL HANDICAP

The rating each golfer is given by sanctioned golf associations.

INSIDE OUT

When a player swings the club down from the top of the swing on the inside of an imaginary line passing through the ball to the target.

IRON

A narrow club. Used for both short and long shots.

LAG

To putt a golf ball so it is left close to the hole.

LIE

The position of the ball on the fairway.

LINE UP

The position a golfer takes when considering the placement of the ball and the direction of the target.

LOW BALL

The ball in a four-ball match that has the lowest handicap strokes. The other competitors are allowed to use handicap strokes equal to the difference between their handicap and that of the low ball.

Also, a term often used when referring to the ball in a group of players that has the lowest score for a hole. It can be either the gross or net score.

MARKER

A small flat object used to mark the spot where the ball is sitting on the putting green. With the marker in place you can then pick up the ball to remove it from the path of an oncoming ball or to clean it before you putt.

MATCH PLAY

Scoring each hole as an individual unit, the player who has won the most holes wins the match. Gross or net score can be played.

MEDAL PLAY

(See Stroke Play)

MONSTER DAY

A day of golf in which the holes on the greens are placed in the most difficult spots possible.

MULLIGAN

The option on the tee to hit a second ball. On exercising this option, the player is obligated to play the second ball.

NASSAU

A form of gambling normally associated with Four Ball Match Play. Bets are on who will win the front side, back side, and 18.

NET

The total number of strokes on a hole or 18 holes less the handicap.

NINETEENTH HOLE

When finishing 18 holes, golfers will often stop for refreshment. This is called the 19th hole.

OUT OF BOUNDS

The area designated out of the playing zone and marked by white stakes.

OVER THE TOP

When a player swings down from outside in, hitting over the top of the golf ball.

PAR

The number of strokes designated to use on a particular hole. For example, a player is either strokes over or under par, or even par.

PENALTY

Strokes added to a player's score for the infraction of rules.

PIN

The pole that holds the flag, indicating the position of the cup on the putting green. The pole or stick is approximately 8 feet long.

PITCH

A shot hit to the green, close to the hole. A "pitch" shot trajectory is high in the air, as opposed to a "chip" shot.

PITCH AND PUTT

When a ball has not reached the green in regulation, the player can "pitch" on and "putt" in for a par.

PITCH AND RUN

A high soft shot from near the green. The intention is for the ball to roll to the hole. Usually a higher shot with less roll than a Chip and Run.

POLIE

An approach shot with an iron from the fairway that ends up within the length of the flagstick.

POST

To record your golf score for the day.

POSTING SHEET

The document on which you record your golf score for the day.

PRESS

When a player or team starts a new bet after being 2 down on the original bet. Example: The first bet is still going on. A zero is put on the score card to remind the players that another bet has started. The zero is put on the score card at the hole where the player said "PRESS". NOTE: Anytime a PRESS is added, existing bets are still enforced. The option to accept or not accept PRESS is sometimes agreed to on the first tee.

PULL

When a player hits the ball to the left of his intended line as the result of an outside-in swing.

PUSH

When players tie on a hole. Also, sometimes used to refer to a shot that is slightly to the right of the target as a result of not finishing the swing properly.

PUTT

The stroke used to hit the ball into the hole on the putting green.

PUTTER

A club with a flat face. Used on the putting green.

RED STAKE

Used to indicate a water hazard.

RINGER

A golfer who is very often a winner. (Sandbagger)

ROUGH

The long grass along the fairway or putting green.

ROUND

A term for 18 holes of golf.

SAND

Material used in a bunker or sand trap. Also used to dress a green.

SAND TRAP

A sand pit used to increase the difficulty of landing a ball on the green or as an obstacle along a fairway.

SANDBAG

To play better than your handicap indicates.

SANDBAGGER

A golfer who plays better than he has led people to believe.

SANDED

The condition of the greens when they are aerated, covered with sand, and the excess sand brushed off.

SANDIE

A par that is made after the golf ball has been in the sand trap.

SANDING THE GREEN

The process of placing a layer of sand and organic material on a green to smooth the surface.

SCOTCH

A game in which players alternate hitting the same ball (See Games: Scotch)

SCRAMBLE

A game in which each player hits a ball from the position of the best ball from tee to green, resulting in one score for the team. (See Games: Scramble)

SCRAMBLERS

Players who miss a green in regulation but manage to score par on a hole.

SCRATCH

Designation of a golfer who has a zero (0) handicap.

SCULL

Striking the ball in the center with the leading edge of an iron. The ball rolls on the ground or may get up in the air only slightly.

SHAFT

The metal, wood or graphite rod that makes up a golf club, with a club head on one end and a grip on the other.

SHANK

When a ball is hit with the hozel of the club.

SHIFT

The movement or change of weight from one side of the body to the other.

SHOT

The result of hitting the golf ball with the golf club. i.e., That was a good shot.

SHOTGUN

A tournament in which all contestants tee off at the same time. The players are sent to various holes on the golf course and given the same tee off time.

SIDE HILL

The position of the golf ball when resting on the side of a hill.

SINK

To stroke the ball into the hole on the putting green.

SKINS

A skin is awarded to a player for having the lowest score on a hole. No skin is awarded for ties.

SKY BALL

A golf ball that goes extremely higher than necessary or expected.

SLICE

A ball that veers sharply right (left for a left-hander) after it is hit.

SLICER

A golfer who hits a slice.

SLOPE

Refers to a handicapping procedure that shows how a difficult golf course can affect a player's handicap. The basic concept is: the tougher the course, the steeper the slope rating. This is designed to make handicaps more equitable for golfers of all abilities.

When the Southern and Northern California Golf Associations introduce Slope into their system on January 1, 1990, the index will be the biggest single change in handicapping.

Thousands of words have been written about Slope in the past few years, but the simple fact is that 99% of the golfers in both associations will have to know only two things about Slope: "Each will have to know his index and how to covert it into a handicap when he plays at any course."

What is the index? The index is a mathematical calculation which is always expressed in a decimal and, with one exception is never used for play. The number represents each golfer's playing ability on a 113-Slope golf course, a course of standard difficulty. If a golfer were to play every round on a 113-Slope golf course, his index and his playing handicap would be the same. But since golfers play courses of widely varying difficulties, the Slope system mathematically converts those differentials into a number that assumes all scores <u>were</u> shot on a 113-Slope course.

How do I use my index? Each time you go to a course with a Slope rating (as of 1990 in California, virtually all courses will be rated), convert your index into a playing handicap by checking a chart posted at the course. Example: You're playing a course in which the back tees have a Slope rating of 130. If your index is 11.2, you'd find that number in the range that says 10.9 to 11.7 meaning you would play to a 13 handicap. If your index is 16.3, you'd find your number in the range that says 16.1 to 16.9 and would play to a 19 handicap from this set of tees.

That's all you need to know about Slope: Your index and how to convert it into a handicap.

Golfers will continue to post scores exactly as they have done in the past, with the exception that out-of-state posting sheets will now require both a course and a Slope rating. The SCGA's computer system will automatically convert all differentials into indexes, which will be distributed to clubs in the same manner as now occurs with monthly handicaps.

The only time a golfer would play to his index is if he competes on a course without a Slope rating. When California goes on Slope, however, only four small associations around the country will not be using the system.

The key to Slope is simple: Think Index!

SPRAY

A term used to describe shots that are hit everywhere on the playing area except on the fairway.

STAKED TREE

Any tree or shrub tied to a stake. If a ball is unplayable because the staked tree is interfering with the game, the player is allowed a free drop.

STANCE

The position of the body when the golfer is ready to hit the ball.

STOBBIE

An approach shot to the green which lands by the flagstick, within the length of the putter head.

STROKE

Any attempt to hit the ball is considered a stroke.

STROKE PLAY

Competition between players in which the winner plays the stipulated round or rounds with the fewest strokes.

STROKES AS THEY FALL

The strokes are the handicap strokes a player is entitled to in a match or competition. They are applied to a player's score on a hole by hole basis to determine a player's net score for each hole.

SWING

A term used to describe the act of striking the golf ball.

SYNDICATE

A group of people who buy a player in a Calcutta.

TEE

A small wooden object used to hold the golf ball. It is only used on the first shot (or tee box) of each hole.

TEE BOX

The area where the player tees up the golf ball to start play on each hole. Also referred to as The Tee.

TEND

To stand at the flag stick while a person is putting so you can pull out "the flag" before the ball reaches the hole.

THIN

Not hitting under the ball or not striking the ball squarely.

TIJUANA

(See Games: Tijuana)

TIJUANA SCRAMBLE

A team of players all tee off and select the best positioned ball. All hit a shot from that position. Continue until the ball is holed. Gross score.

TOP/TOPPED/TOPPING

Striking the ball on the top with the leading edge of a club.

TOUR

Organized golf play for professional golfers.

TRAP

A sand or grass pit that is placed along the fairway or around the putting green to increase the difficulty of play.

UNPLAYABLE

Refers to a ball that rests in a spot that makes it impossible to hit. The ball may be moved and the player assessed a penalty stroke.

UP AND DOWN

A term used when a player is not on the green in regulation (1 shot for 3 pars, 2 shots for 4 pars, and 3 shots for 5 pars), but chips (up) and makes a one putt (down), scoring par.

UP HILL

The lie or position of the golf ball when it is above the golfer's feet.

WATER HOLE

Any water that the player has to consider before making a shot. Lakes, creeks, etc. are used to increase the difficulty of play.

WHALIE

A player who saves par on a hole after being in the water.

WHIFF/WHIFFING

Attempting to hit the ball and missing it.

WHITE STAKE

Indicates the out-of-bounds area on each hole. If a golf ball comes to rest outside the white stakes, the player is assessed a two-stroke penalty and must replay the ball from where it was hit before it went out of bounds.

"WHO'S AWAY OR OUT"

This term refers to the player who is farthest from the hole and therefore has the right to hit next. It is most often used on the green to determine the order for putting.

WINTER RULES

Allows a player to lift, clean, and place his ball near its original position, when adverse conditions make it otherwise impossible for play to continue on an equal basis for all players.

WOOD

A club with an oval shape, originally made of wood. Used for longer shots.

WORM BURNER

A ball that stays close to the ground after being hit.

YELLOW STAKES

Stakes used to define a water hazard.

BETTING

Cash

CHAPTER 3

BETTING

BETTING ON THE PROS

The draft system can be used by drawing from a deck of cards. The highest card picks first, second highest picks next, and so on. A point system is used to determine the winner and the amount. In addition, decide on the amounts paid for eagle, birdie, bogey and double and triple bogey. For example, if your golfer makes an eagle, the other players in the game owe you $20. If he makes a birdie, they owe you $5. Par has no value, but if your golfer shoots a bogey, you owe everyone $5, $10 for a double bogey, and $20 for a triple bogey.

Use one suit from a deck of cards: for instance, all the hearts except the king. Twelve players draw from the hearts for selection of their professional golfer. The player drawing the ace has first selection, the deuce second selection and on up through the queen for final selections. The player who selects last is left with the balance of the players in the field, if they have not yet been chosen. The 12 players put an agreed upon amount into the pot before the professionals begin their play. Winner takes all.

BINGO, BANGO, BONGO

A dollar amount is established for first on the putting green, closest to the hole, and first in the hole. A variation of this bet is to double the bet if one player wins all three bets. Another variation is to triple the bet if one player wins all three bets with a birdie.

BOGIED?

The first player to shoot a bogey automatically owes the other players a pre-determined amount. He owes them that same amount for each following hole until another player shoots a bogey. The new bogey player continues until a new bogey is made by another player.

BONG

An amount is established for *Bong* points. *Bongs* are mishaps that occur during a round of golf. The player with the highest number of *Bong* points at the end of 18 holes owes the others the difference in their points and his.

Bongs	Assessment
Whiff	4
Teeing off in front of marker	1
Lost ball	2
Out of bounds	2
In sand trap	1
In the water	1
Two strokes in the sand trap	3
Three strokes in the sand trap	5
Hitting one trap to another	2
Three putt	2
Four putt	3

BY THE YARD

Winners are determined by the length of the holes that they win. A player who wins a hole 200 yards longer than his opponent wins 200 points. Each point is valued at a penny, nickel or dime, depending on the player's pocketbook.

CAN AND CAN'T

A player declares he can make a difficult shot, and the opponent says he can't. A bet is entered into. One variation: a player bets that for a specified amount he will shoot his average score and will double that amount if he shoots lower. Another variation is for a team to win or lose a specified amount if they don't shoot par or if they win the hole.

CHOKE

The last golfer to three-putt a green owes the other players the pre-determined amount established for each hole. Players decide before playing whether a putter used off the green is "or is not" a putt.

A variation is to double the bet if two players are three-putting or to triple the bet if three players are three-putting, etc.

Choke

CLOSEST TO THE HOLE

The player who lands closest to the hole wins a predetermined amount from each player. A variation to is to cancel the bet if the player closest to the hole three-putts.

GIMME'S

A player calls out "Gimme", usually for a short putt (two to five feet) he thinks can be made. The opponent has the option of giving him the putt or making the player putt out. If the opponent makes the player putt out, and the putt is made, the bet on that hole is doubled. If the putt is missed, the player only loses the amount bet on the hole.

HAMMER

A golfer at any time during play may call out, "hammer". If the opponent accepts the "hammer", the established bet is automatically doubled, and play resumes. If the opponent does not accept the "hammer", the bet is automatically cancelled, and a new bet is established for the next hole.

HI-LO TOURNAMENT

There are three parts to this tournament.

The Teams: The 120 participants are divided into "high" and "low" handicap groups of 60 each. Each team is formed by a blind draw of one player from each group, until 60 teams have been formed.

The Official (main) Tournament: This tournament is for prizes, glory, and honor. For scoring, use the better-ball score of each team, using full handicaps.

The Buy-Out Harry Hotshot (10) and Danny Dubber (25) have been drawn as a team and are being auctioned. The official total handicap of the team is 35 (10+25). The bidding begins. Bidder A offers "32," meaning he is willing to give up 3 handicap strokes in order to own the team. Bidder B offers "30". Bidder C bids "27". Finally, Bidder X (Monty Martini) bids "21". The bidding stops;

no one is willing to bid lower. Monty is now the proud owner of the Hotshot-Dubber team and has paid $100 plus a "premium" of plus 14—the official total handicap of 35 less his bid of 21.

Let's suppose that the Hotshot–Dubber team turns in a better-ball score of 61-64 (a total of 125) in the Official Tournament, using full handicaps, of course. Their score in the Sweeps Tournament would be 125 plus the "premium" paid of +14, or 139. Consequently, the winners of the Official Tournament and the winners of the Sweeps generally are not the same team, although it is possible.

Each team member has the option of buying 25% of his own team by paying the owner $25 before tee-off time. Also, each member may bid on his own team in open bidding.

On occasion, a player will fail to show up. In that event, that team is eliminated from the Sweeps Tournament, the owner is reimbursed his $100, and the pool is diminished by that amount. If, however, a replacement can be found in time, the "new" team is eligible to compete in the Official Tournament, but not in the Sweeps.

The Pool is divided as follows:

1st Place	25%
2nd Place	17%
3rd Place	12%
4th Place	10%
5th-10th Place	5%
Daily 1st and 2nd Places .	2% and 1%

Ties will share equally the appropriate places.

There is a buy-out pool for those who are interested. The buy-out pool goes to the first ten places in the official event. The cost of the buy-out is $40 per team.

ALL TRANSACTIONS ARE CASH (CHECKS ARE ALSO ACCEPTED). Successful bidders must pay for their team(s) at the conclusion of the auction. Payoff is at the conclusion of play.

HONORS

The object is to hold honors on the tee as long as possible. Players decide the number of times a player or team has to hold tee to win the bet . . . six or nine, for example. A toss of the coin decides who tees off first.

LOW BALL

One of the most popular betting games. Player with lowest score on the hole wins the hole.

ON TARGET

This side bet is started before play begins by each golfer writing on a slip of paper the score he will shoot. The scores are kept secret until play is finished. Any team or golfer who calls his score correctly wins outright. Ties split the pot. Any golfer who has a double bogey or higher on holes 17 or 18 may not win the bet. This prevents a golfer from deliberately adding strokes to his score to win the bet.

ON THE BEACH

One player bets another that the first player's next shot will land in the sand trap. If this bet is accepted and the ball does not go in, the first player receives three times the specified amount. Should the ball go into the trap, the player owes the challenger two times the amount of the bet.

PRACTICE PLACING PUTTS

This game is for the practice putting green. The player whose ball is farthest from the hole putts next, as in regulation play. The difference is that the previous players' balls are not marked, consequently setting up an obstacle course. If a putter's ball makes contact with another ball, the player automatically loses the hole, owes the other players the pre-determined amount bet, and is forced to putt last on the next hole.

On Target

PRESS

A press means a new bet. If a player is losing by one or more strokes, another bet or "press" can be made. Generally, a player cannot press unless he is down two strokes, but it can be specified that one down press will be the wager. On the last hole (if agreed upon before playing), a player may want to bet a "press" to get even. This bet does not have to be accepted.

PUTT? I CAN

This is a side-betting game. Any player may challenge another on the green by betting that he will three-putt the green. The challenged player may accept or reject the bet. If the bet is accepted and the challenged player does not three-putt, that player wins three times the amount of the bet. If he does three-putt, the challenger wins two times the bet. (This will improve your putting).

ROLL 'EM

This bet can be doubled only twice during a round of golf and only when the losing team calls out, "roll 'em". "Roll 'Em" can be called before the opposing team tees off or when a ball is in the air, but not after the ball hits the ground. This bet cannot be rejected by the winning team.

SCOTCH

A dollar amount is established for points. Each hole has a five point possibility: two for the low ball, one for the low total (with handicap), one for closest to the pin, and one for natural birdies. If all five points are won by one player, the bet is doubled. A variation of this bet is to award two points for low score, one point for closest to the pin, one point for a natural birdie, and one point for a sandy par.

SHORT

For a pre-determined amount, a player is penalized for leaving a putt short if the putt would have won or tied the hole.

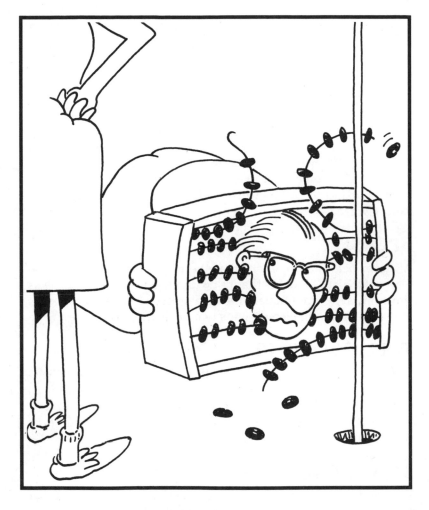

*How did I know it was
too much a hole?*

SKINS

Each hole is given a point value. The player with the low score is awarded the point for each hole. In a tie, the points are carried over to the next hole. In betting, each point is awarded a monetary value.

SKINS VARIATION

Each player contributes a designated amount to the pot. The golfer with the lowest score on a hole gets credit for a skin. Ties are simply ties and do not accumulate. A natural bird is worth two skins. When the round is over, divide the number of skins into the pot to determine the value of each skin (i.e., the pot is worth $20 and five skins were made during the round, so each skin is worth $4).

SPLASH

A player bets the opponent that the next shot will go into the water. If the player makes the shot without getting wet, he collects three times the amount bet. If the player goes "Splash" and lands in the water, the challenger wins two times the amount bet.

TALLY THE PUTTS

Each putt is given a value. The putts for each player are "tallied" at the completion of the round of golf. Bets are paid according to the difference in the number of putts per player. For example: a golfer with 45 putts owes the player with 36 putts nine points or the amount pre-determined for each putt.

THREE TWO MANY

Each golfer is allowed to three-putt two holes. If he exceeds that number a predetermined amount is owed to the other players for each three-putt hole.

THREESOME

Involves three players. Each hole is worth nine points, and a value is given for each point. The winner of the hole receives five points,

(Continued on next page)

Toughie? Go for it Gorilla!

the runner-up receives three points, and the loser receives one point. In the event of a tie for first place, the points are distributed four, four, and one. In a second place tie, the points are distributed five for the winner and two for the two players who placed second. Add up the points at the finish of play, and multiply by the predetermined value. Subtract the loser's points from the winner's for the payoff.

TOO MUCH A HOLE!

This bet varies according to your comfort zone! Using five cents per hole, playing low ball, the payoff looks like this.

Hole	Pays	Hole	Pays
1	.05	10	25.60
2	.10	11	51.20
3	.20	12	102.40
4	.40	13	204.80
5	.80	14	409.60
6	1.60	15	819.20
7	3.20	16	1638.40
8	6.40	17	3276.80
9	12.80	18	6553.60

This bet doubles on every hole, and you play carry overs! Try a penny a hole—it does add up!

TOUGHIE (OR, GO FOR IT GORILLA)

One player may challenge another player anywhere on the course that he cannot make the next shot. This challenge may be accepted or rejected. If accepted, the player must go for the shot. If the shot is made, the player receives three times the amount of the bet. If the shot is missed, the challenger receives two times the amount of the bet.

TWENTY-ONE

This game is for the practice putting green. The object is to reach 21 points first, using two putts. Points are made for a one-putt (three points) and closest to the hole (one point). If no putt is made after two putts, the player closest to the hole wins two points. A predetermined amount is established for each point.

RULES FOR SURVIVAL

Golf Etiquette

CHAPTER 4

RULES FOR SURVIVAL

HOW THE LATE HENRY COTTON COPED WITH OLD AGE

Henry Cotton was a famed British player and teacher who won three British Open titles. In later years when he became an honorary member of the Royal Burgess Golfing Society, he took the occasion to list his three methods for coping with his advancing age when on the golf course. They are:

1. I always play from the ladies' tee or, if necessary, farther in front.

2. I never have a bad lie in the rough, because I use the leather mashie, that is, chip it out with my foot.

3. I concede myself all putts on the grounds that I've made thousands of them before and don't need the practice.

HOW TO HANDLE A GOLF CART

Proper handling of a golf cart is essential to course maintenance, pace of play, and personal safety. The following checklist is based on recommendations by the late Fred L. Riggins, Sr., of Port Huron, Michigan.

1. On starting out, check to see if your cart is set to go forward and not backward.

2. Do not start until everyone has driven from the tee.

3. Do not drive ahead of the ball which is closest to the tee. If you have a gasoline cart, turn off the motor while your companion is addressing and playing the ball. Never continue driving when someone is playing a shot.

4. When appropriate, advance to your own ball. Always stop

(Continued on next page)

even with the ball, and park to the side on which your clubs (or your companion's clubs) are carried.

5. Always park reasonably close to the ball so the player can size up his shot, make his selection of clubs, and even change clubs without undue delay.

6. If you have to park a distance from your ball, size up the distance to the green as best as you can. Then take one or two extra clubs with you to save trips back and forth to the cart.

7. When hunting for a lost ball, park your cart in the rough. Don't leave it in the fairway in the way of the next group.

8. When driving a cart, be careful not to injure fairways, greens, or bunkers by driving too close.

9. Never park in front of a green while putting. If possible, park high on the side of the green nearest the next tee, out of the way of the next group.

10. Never drive a cart in muddy places, through puddles of water, or in any place that could be injured.

11. Don't drag your feet outside the cart. Keep them inside until the cart is stopped.

12. Don't get in or out of the cart when it is moving.

13. Don't drive parallel to the top of a hill or rise in such a way that the cart is on a pronounced slant. It might overturn.

14. When ascending or descending, always approach a hill or rise in a straight line. If you want to turn at the bottom of a hill, keep going straight for a time after you have reached the bottom. Then, turn slowly at a big angle.

Slow Play

GOLF ETIQUETTE

Far from being arbitrary or fussy, the rules of etiquette in golf are based on common sense and respect for the course and the play of those around you. They're intended to keep play safe, simple, and, as far as possible, quick.

Based on advice from golf professionals, the following is how to properly conduct your play on a typical hole.

Apart from being familiar with the general rules of golf, you should acquaint yourself with the course layout and the local rules (generally printed on the score card) before you step up to the first tee. It will save time later if a ruling is needed.

As the foursome before you tees off, remain quiet and still until the last person has hit. You must not hit your own tee shot until that foursome has hit its second shot and is out of your range.

Get accustomed to playing "ready golf" when the course is crowded. This means that players tee off when they are ready and not necessarily in the order of "honors" from the last hole.

If your tee shot flies out of bounds or into a water hazard or impenetrable brush, you must hit a second shot from the tee. If you aren't sure if it went out of bounds or whether you'll be able to find it, you should hit a provisional shot from the tee, just in case.

In every instance, the player whose ball is farthest from the hole is the first to hit. If, however, there is a delay (in looking for a ball in the rough, for instance, or retrieving a club), other players may hit out of turn in order to speed the play.

In the fairway, make sure you are about to hit your own ball. Know your ball's make and number, and be able to identify it before hitting it. It is often easy to hit another player's ball by mistake.

You should not walk in front or downrange of a player who is about to hit a shot from the fairway. If another player is in the line of your shot, warn him before hitting, and allow him to get out of the way or stand behind an obstruction, such as a tree. Generally, no player should be downrange from a player about to hit a ball.

Never hit your ball to the green while the foursome in front of you is within range. Wait until they are well off the green before you hit.

If you take a divot on a fairway shot, replace it immediately or apply sand as provided. Scarring occurs quickly if the turf is not packed back down after a shot.

If your shot lands in a bunker, be sure to rake the sand neatly after you hit out, smoothing all ball marks and footprints.

If your shot hits the surface of the green and creates a divot or any mark, it should be repaired immediately. Use a tee or a ball mark repair tool to fluff up the divot and fill in the hole. Tamp it down gently with your foot. If your spikes scratch the putting surface, tamp the scratches flat with your putter or...again, gently...with your foot. Such damage, if left unrepaired, is costly to correct and drives up the price of green fees.

Leave electric golf cars, pull carts, and bags well off the putting surface.

Know where each player's line of putt is. This is the path the ball is likely to take to the cup. Avoid stepping on this line.

If a player asks for the pin to be tended, the player whose ball is closest to the hole usually does it. When the pin is finally removed, it should be laid flat on the green so as not to scar the surface.

As unobtrusively as possible, players not putting should line up their putts so when their turn arrives they can step up to the ball immediately. As on the tee, players should remain silent while others are putting. When everyone has putted out, leave the green

(Continued on next page)

immediately and allow the foursome behind you to hit up. Mark your score cards on the next tee. Keep track of the foursome in front of you and behind you. If you are falling behind the pace of play, make an effort to speed up. You can let the group behind you go in front of you—eliminate **slow play!**

Yell "fore!" and yell it loudly if a ball you have hit is heading toward another golfer.

Always hold your temper. Accept the fact that bad shots and bad rounds are inevitable, even for professionals.

Always remember the 3 P's of golf:

80% of your shots will be *playable*.

10% of your shots will be *poor*.

and

10% of your shots will be *perfect!*

PARTNER SELECTION

For fun and random selection of a partner try some of these methods.

1. Flip a coin.
2. High handicaps together and low handicaps together.
3. High handicap and low handicap together.
4. Cart riders together.
5. Cart partners together.
6. Cart drivers together.
7. One player tosses four golf balls in the air. Two closest together are partners.
8. Each player tosses his ball to the tee marker and the two closest to the tee marker are partners.

INDEX

INDEX

INDEX

INDEX

INDEX

INDEX

INDEX

INDEX

INDEX

INDEX

INDEX

ABOUT THE AUTHORS

Linda Valentine was born in Hollywood, California. Married with a combined family of five children and six grandchildren, she took up golf after playing tennis for many years and says, "I should have started sooner!" She has played golf all over the world and is a tough 17 handicapper. She belongs to Big Canyon Country Club in Newport Beach, California, and is a proud member of the hole-in-one club.

Margie Hubbard is an avid golfer. She has played the game all over the world from Scotland to New Zealand and has won numerous tournaments. Her home course is Big Canyon Country Club in Newport Beach, California, where she maintains a 16 handicap. She lives in Corona del Mar, California.

Improve your game with these comprehensive Perigee golf guides.

Break 100 in 21 Days
A How-to Guide for the Weekend Golfer
by Walter Ostroske and John Devaney
illustrated with over 50 black-and-white photographs
The first easy-to-follow program by a PGA teaching pro for shooting in the 90s and 80s, aimed at the person who plays only ten to twenty times a year.

Correct the 10 Most Common Golf Problems in 10 Days
by Walter Ostroske and John Devaney
illustrated with over 50 black-and-white photographs
The first book to pinpoint and correct the ten most common problems in golfers' swings—in just ten days.

Two-Putt Greens in 18 Days
A How-to Guide for the Weekend Golfer
by Walter Ostroske and John Devaney
illustrated with over 50 black-and-white photographs
An easy-to-use daily program for mastering good putting in just eighteen days.

Golf Games Within the Game
200 Fun Ways Players Can Add Variety and Challenge to Their Game
by Linda Valentine and Margie Hubbard
illustrated with over 25 line drawings
A one-of-a-kind collection of games and bets for added excitement on the golf course, culled from members of more than 8,000 golf clubs across America.

The Whole Golf Catalog
by Rhonda Glenn and Robert R. McCord
illustrated with line drawings and photographs
Lists professional and amateur golf associations, golf museums and archives, instruction camps and tours, sources of golf merchandise, a calendar of important events, and much more.

Golf Rules in Pictures
An Official Publication of the United States Golf Association
introduction by Arnold Palmer
Clearly captioned pictures cover all the rules of golf: scoring, clubs, procedure, hazards, and penalty strokes. Includes the official text of The Rules of Golf approved by the U.S. Golf Association and the Royal and Ancient Golf Club of St. Andrews, Scotland.

Golf Techniques in Pictures
by Michael Brown
illustrated with over 100 line drawings
Chock-full of both fundamental and advanced techniques, this is the most complete handbook for successful swinging, putting, and chipping.

These books are available at your local bookstore or wherever books are sold. Ordering is also easy and convenient. Just call 1-800-631-8571 or send your order to:

The Putnam Publishing Group
390 Murray Hill Parkway, Dept. B
East Rutherford, NJ 07073

_____ Break 100 in 21 Days	399-51600-X	$8.95	$11.75
_____ Correct the 10 Most Common Golf			
Problems in 10 Days	399-51656-5	8.95	11.75
_____ Two-Putt Greens in 18 Days	399-51747-2	8.95	11.75
_____ Golf Games Within the Game	399-51762-6	8.95	11.75
_____ The Whole Golf Catalog	399-51623-9	15.95	20.95
_____ Golf Rules in Pictures	399-51438-4	7.95	10.50
_____ Golf Techniques in Pictures	399-51664-6	7.95	10.50

Subtotal $_____

Postage and handling* $_____

Sales tax (CA, NJ, NY, PA) $_____

Total Amount Due $_____

Payable in U.S. funds (no cash orders accepted). $10.00 minimum for credit card orders.
*Postage and handling: $2.00 for 1 book, 50¢ for each additional book up to a maximum of $4.50.

Enclosed is my ☐ check ☐ money order
Please charge my ☐ Visa ☐ MasterCard ☐ American Express

Card # _____ Expiration date _____

Signature as on charge card _____

Name _____

Address _____

City _____ State _____ Zip _____

Please allow six weeks for delivery. Prices subject to change without notice.